Books written by Jack Hartman

Trust God for Your Finances
What Will Heaven Be Like?
Never, Never G...
How to Study th...
Quiet Confidence
One Hundred Years ,
Nuggets of Faith

Books co-authored with Judy Hartman

Reverent Awe of God
God's Plan for Your Life
You Can Hear the Voice of God
God's Instructions for Growing Older
Effective Prayer
Overcoming Fear
A Close and Intimate Relationship with God
God's Joy Regardless of Circumstances
Victory Over Adversity
What Does God Say?
Receive Healing from the Lord
Unshakable Faith in Almighty God
Exchange Your Worries for God's Perfect Peace
God's Wisdom Is Available to You
Increased Energy and Vitality

Scripture Meditation Cards
co-authored by Jack and Judy Hartman

Receive Healing from the Lord
Freedom from Worry and Fear
Enjoy God's Wonderful Peace
God Is Always with You
Continually Increasing Faith in God
Receive God's Blessings in Adversity
Financial Instructions from God
Find God's Will for Your Life
A Closer Relationship with the Lord
Our Father's Wonderful Love

Reverent Awe of God

Jack and Judy Hartman

Lamplight Ministries, Inc., Dunedin, Florida

We are excited that you have chosen to read this book. Our prayer is that you will be gripped by the Word of God that is contained in it. We pray that God Himself will speak to your heart and that you will come to know and live in the reverent awe of God.

We would like to hear from you. Please send us an email at lamplightmin@yahoo.com or drop us a note at Lamplight Ministries, Inc., P.O. Box 1307, Dunedin FL 34697. Please visit our website at www.lamplight.net and tell us if this book has helped you.

You also can request our free monthly newsletter by mail or email. We would be so pleased to stay in touch with you with our newsletter. You can see updates on forthcoming books and keep us in prayer as we pray for you. You also can receive a daily devotional from a set of our Scripture Meditation Cards. You can download the first chapter of each of our books.

Jack and Judy

Copyright 2013

Jack and Judy Hartman

Jack and Judy Hartman

Lamplight Ministries Inc.

PO Box 1307

Dunedin, Florida 34697-2921

Telephone: 1-800-540-1597

FAX: 1-727-784-2980

Website: lamplight.net

Email: lamplightmin@yahoo.com

Facebook: facebook.com/jackandjudylamplight

Twitter: twitter.com/lamplightmin

Blog: lamplightmin.wordpress.com

Ebooks: Go to smashwords.com.
Type in "Jack and Judy Hartman"

ISBN: 978-0-915445-28-8

Library of Congress Control Number: 2013922172

Dedication

We dedicate this book to Christopher Mulapwa who is the director of Elohim Global Ministries in Zambia. Christopher went into the ministry immediately after completing high school. He subsequently graduated with a diploma in theology from a theological college in South Africa. Christopher also serves as pastor of Christian Revival Church which contains a training center for church members who have never been to Bible college.

Christopher's wife Veronica also is a graduate of a theological college. She directs the youth ministry in their church. Their future vision is to form a theological college, to plant churches in cities and towns in Zambia and to build educational centers for underprivileged children in Zambia. Christopher and Veronica have three children, Marvellous, Zoe and Shalom.

We communicate by email with Christopher several times each month. Christopher and Veronica often use our books in their church. We are so pleased that God has brought us together with these committed Christians in Zambia.

Table of Contents

Introduction

How many sermons have you heard on the fear of God? How many books have you read pertaining to the fear of God? Very little has been taught on the fear of God. However, as you go through this book, we believe that you will find that the fear of God is a vitally important topic. We believe that your life will be changed immensely if you learn and obey God's specific instructions on this subject.

We have chosen the title *Reverent Awe of God* because we believe that these words are an accurate description of the fear of God. When you fear God, you revere Him for Who He is. You are in absolute awe of Him. We will explain in detail the incredible blessings that God promises to His children who fear Him with reverent awe.

You will see that God promises long life, deliverance from your enemies and supernatural protection to each of His children who fear Him with reverent awe. You will see that God promises to help you, to meet all of your needs and to teach and guide you if you truly fear Him. This short list contains only a few of the blessings that God promises to each of His children who will learn and obey His instructions pertaining to reverent awe for Him.

We believe that this book will contain a great deal of scriptural information that many readers have not considered. We pray that you will approach the scriptural contents of this book with a humble and teachable attitude. God does not want you to make His scriptural teachings ineffective because you think in a traditional worldly manner (see Matthew 15:6). We pray that you will approach this book with an open mind to scriptural instructions that you may not have known previously.

We now use *The Amplified Bible* almost exclusively in our books. I (Jack) have been using *The Amplified Bible* since 1975. At that time only *The Amplified New Testament* was available. I bought this version of the Bible when I saw it in a Christian bookstore because of an inscription from Dr. Billy Graham on the cover. Dr. Graham said, "This is the best Study Testament on the market. It is a magnificent translation. I use it constantly."

The Amplified Bible is the result of the study of a group of Bible scholars who spent a total of more than 20,000 hours amplifying the Bible. They believe that traditional word-by-word translation often fails to reveal the shades of meaning that are part of the original Greek, Hebrew and Aramaic biblical texts.

Any amplification of the original text uses brackets for words that clarify the meaning and parentheses for words that contain additional phrases included in the original language. Through this amplification the reader will gain a better understanding of what Hebrew and Greek listeners instinctively understood.

We would like to give you a specific example of *why* we use *The Amplified Bible* almost exclusively.
- "I can do all things through Christ which strengtheneth me." (Philippians 4:13, *The King James Version*)
- "I can do all this through him who gives me strength." (Philippians 4:13, *The New International Version*)

· "I have strength for all things in Christ Who empowers me [I am ready for anything and equal to anything through Him Who infuses inner strength into me; I am self-sufficient in Christ's sufficiency]." (Philippians 4:13, *The Amplified Bible*)

Please note the significant amplification of the original Greek in *The Amplified Bible*. If you desire to meditate on Philippians 4:13, you will find that there is much more depth of meaning in *The Amplified Bible* version of this verse. All Scripture references in this book are from *The Amplified Bible*.

As you read this book, we recommend that you highlight or underline all passages of Scripture that are meaningful to you and our explanation of this Scripture if it is helpful to you. Write notes in the margin or at the top or bottom of the page. If you do, you then will be able to go back through this book after you have read it the first time. You will be able to *meditate* on the meaningful passages of Scripture that you already have identified (see Joshua 1:8 and Psalm 1:2-3).

I (Jack) want to explain why I use the first person on many occasions in our books. I write the first two drafts of each book. Judy then adds her valuable input to the next two drafts. I then write the final two drafts.

I do not want to use the words "I (Jack)" every time that I use a first-person reference. I will just use the word "I" whenever I make a personal observation during the remainder of this book. Any personal observations from Judy will be clearly identified.

We blend together our explanations of Scripture. We thank God for the high privilege of dividing His Word, each of us bringing different expertise to create a final book for you. Imagine a husband and wife, each with an office at home, working together every day with different viewpoints that

God brings together harmoniously. We are very grateful that God has used us in this way for many years.

Every principle that we will explain in this book is solidly anchored on Scripture. We explain each passage of Scripture in simple and easy-to-understand language. We pray that the scriptural contents of this book and our explanation of this Scripture will help *you* to learn valuable scriptural truth pertaining to reverent awe for God.

Chapter 1

God is Great, Awesome and Majestic

The Bible speaks often of the fear of God. When you fear God, you hold Him in reverent awe at all times. The word "reverent" means an attitude of deep respect and love for God Who is sacred and holy. When we speak of awe of God, we refer to His grandeur and His majesty.

In this book we will carefully study what the Bible teaches about the grandeur of God. The more that you know about the majesty of God, the more reverence and awe you will have for Him. You will turn more and more away from personal desires and the attractions of the world to give God the reverence and awe that He deserves.

We will begin our study of the grandeur of God by looking at the universe that God created. Many people think primarily in terms of the world. The truth is that the earth where we live is merely one of innumerable planets in the universe. The Bible speaks of the God of the universe "Who made [the constellations] the Bear, Orion, and the [loose cluster] Pleiades, and the [vast starry] spaces of the south; Who does great things past finding out, yes, marvelous things without number." (Job 9:9-10)

Astronomers know that there are trillions of stars in the universe. There are *so many* stars that astronomers cannot even begin to count the exact number of stars. God in His infinite intelligence not only knows the exact number of stars that He created, but He also has a name for *every one* of the trillions of stars. "He determines and counts the number of the stars; He calls them all by their names. Great is our Lord and of great power; His understanding is inexhaustible and boundless." (Psalm 147:4-5)

God has a divine order for everything He has created. The ocean tides come in and go out each day on a definite schedule. The sun rises and sets at a specific time each day. The moon goes through four phases each month. How can you not be in awe of God Who created all of the planets in the universe and directs everything in the universe with such precision?

The magnitude of God's power is beyond the limitations of human comprehension. "Alas, Lord God! Behold, You have made the heavens and the earth by Your great power and by Your outstretched arm! There is nothing too hard or too wonderful for You" (Jeremiah 32:17)

God Who created the heavens and the earth is omnipotent. No problem is too difficult for Him to solve. Our limited human understanding cannot even begin to comprehend how great, awesome and magnificent God is. "Great is the Lord and highly to be praised; and His greatness is [so vast and deep as to be] unsearchable." (Psalm 145:3)

The Bible contains many passages of Scripture that speak of the grandeur of God. "Yours, O Lord, is the greatness and the power and the glory and the victory and the majesty, for all that is in the heavens and the earth is Yours; Yours is the kingdom, O Lord, and Yours it is to be exalted as Head over all. Both riches and honor come from You, and You reign over all. In Your hands are power and might; in Your hands it is to make great and to give strength to all." (I Chronicles 29:11-12)

God is so great, powerful and majestic that He created everything in the universe. He reigns over everyone and everything in the universe. God has all power and might. "…O Lord, God of our fathers, are You not God in heaven? And do You not rule over all the kingdoms of the nations? In Your hand are power and might, so that none is able to withstand You." (II Chronicles 20:6)

God's power, might and majesty are indescribable. Nothing can compare to the awesome holiness, glory and splendor of Almighty God. God said, "I have counsel and sound knowledge, I have understanding, I have might and power. By me kings reign and rulers decree justice. By me princes rule, and nobles, even all the judges and governors of the earth." (Proverbs 8:14-16)

God is in complete control of everyone and everything on earth and everything throughout the universe. "…Blessed be the name of God forever and ever! For wisdom and might are His! He changes the times and the seasons; He removes kings and sets up kings. He gives wisdom to the wise and knowledge to those who have understanding! He reveals the deep and secret things; He knows what is in the darkness, and the light dwells with Him!" (Daniel 2:20-22)

God determines the 24 hours of each day. He determines when the seasons change from winter to summer to fall and to spring. God has complete authority over all human beings who are in positions of government leadership. God knows everything that is taking place throughout the entire universe.

The apostle Paul prayed that the Ephesians would understand the immensity of God's power when he spoke of "…the immeasurable and unlimited and surpassing greatness of His power in and for us who believe, as demonstrated in the working of His mighty strength, Which He exerted in Christ when He raised Him from the dead and seated Him at His [own] right hand in the heavenly [places]" (Ephesians 1:19-20)

God is *so* mighty and so powerful that He was able to reach down to earth to raise His beloved Son Jesus Christ from the dead. God then seated Jesus at His right hand in heaven.

God is omnipotent – He is all-powerful. He is omnipresent – He is able to be in an infinite number of places at the same time. He is omniscient – He knows every minute detail pertaining to every one of the billions of people on earth.

The psalmist David spoke of the omniscience of God when he said, "O Lord, you have searched me [thoroughly] and have known me. You know my downsitting and my uprising; You understand my thought afar off. You sift and search out my path and my lying down, and You are acquainted with all my ways. For there is not a word in my tongue [still unuttered], but, behold, O Lord, You know it altogether." (Psalm 139:1-4)

God knows when you go to sleep each night and when you wake up. He knows every thought of every one of the billions of people in the world. God knows every word that you speak. He even knows what you will say before you speak.

The more that you comprehend the awesome magnitude of Who God truly is, the more you will hold Him in constant and reverent awe. No matter how much we study about God's greatness, we cannot even begin to comprehend His magnificence. There is nothing that God does not know. The omniscience of God is so great that He knows exactly how many hairs you have on your head and how many hairs are on the head of every person in the world. Jesus Christ said, "...even the very hairs of your head are all numbered." (Matthew 10:30)

There is *nothing* about any person in the world that God does not know. "...the Lord searches all hearts and minds and understands all the wanderings of the thoughts...." (I Chronicles 28:9)

Think about the immensity of God Who fully understands every thought of every one of the billions of people in the world. How can you not be in continual awe of God Who is *so* great and *so* magnificent? The psalmist David said, "When I view and consider Your heavens, the work of Your fingers, the moon and the stars, which You have ordained and established, what is man that You are mindful of him, and the son of [earthborn] man that You care for him?" (Psalm 8:3-4)

Even though God created everyone and everything in the universe, He is very interested in *you*. God loves you so much that He said, "...though the mountains should depart and the hills be shaken or removed, yet My love and kindness shall not depart from you..." (Isaiah 54:10)

In this chapter we have done our best to explain what the Bible teaches about the God of the universe. Now that we have studied several verses of Scripture pertaining to the greatness of God, we will devote the next chapter to a detailed scriptural explanation of the fact that God actually lives in your heart if Jesus Christ is your Savior.

Chapter 2

Almighty God Lives in Your Heart

Are you in absolute awe of God after reading the Scripture references in the last chapter? We pray that this chapter and subsequent chapters will help you even more to center every aspect of your life around God Who is so great, mighty and magnificent.

You saw at the end of the last chapter that the psalmist David expressed his wonder at the fact that the same God Who created the heaven, moon and stars cares deeply about each of us. "Anyone who confesses (acknowledges, owns) that Jesus is the Son of God, God abides (lives, makes His home) in him and he [abides, lives, makes his home] in God." (I John 4:15)

The word "anyone" in this verse of Scripture includes you if you have received Jesus Christ as your Savior. God makes His home in your heart. You are instructed to abide constantly in God. If you are not certain that Jesus Christ is your Savior, please stop now and carefully read the Appendix beginning on page 115.

How can you not be in reverent awe of God if you are *certain* that the same God Who created heaven and earth, the moon, the stars and all of the planets and galaxies lives in *your* heart? God is great enough to do all of the things that we explained in Chapter 1, but He lives in the heart of *every* person on earth who has received Jesus Christ as his or her Savior.

God is omnipresent. He is not limited to sitting on His throne in heaven. "One God and Father of [us] all, Who is above all [Sovereign over all], pervading all and [living] in [us] all." (Ephesians 4:6)

This verse explains that God in heaven is above everyone and everything on earth. The amplification explains that He is the sovereign ruler over everything on earth. This verse says that God *pervades all*. The word "pervades" means that God is spread out throughout the universe. The same God Who created heaven and earth and all of the planets and galaxies of the universe is spread out throughout the entire world. God is omnipresent.

Just think of the magnitude of the Scripture that we have studied so far in this chapter. The God of the universe lives in your heart if Jesus Christ is your Savior. You will live a joyous life of constant reverence and awe of God if you are continually conscious that Almighty God lives inside of you.

Ephesians 4:6 refers to God as being your Father. Not only does the God of the universe make His permanent home in your heart, but He also is your loving Father. You are His beloved child. "See what [an incredible] quality of love the Father has given (shown, bestowed on) us, that we should [be permitted to] be named and called and counted the children of God! And so we are!..." (I John 3:1)

Is Jesus Christ your Savior? If He is, you can be certain that the God of the universe is *your* loving Father. When you think of God, think of Him as your loving Father Who makes His home in your heart.

The Scripture that we are studying in the first two chapters of this book is mind-boggling. If Jesus Christ is your Savior, you have supernatural power in your heart that is greater than thermonuclear power or any other power on earth. "The Lord your God is in the midst of you, a Mighty One..." (Zephaniah 3:17)

This verse says that God is in the midst of you. God is so mighty and powerful that there is nothing that He cannot do. The Bible speaks of Christians being "...filled [through all your being] unto all the fullness of God [may have the richest measure of the divine Presence, and become a body wholly filled and flooded with God Himself]!" (Ephesians 3:19)

If your life is centered around a continual consciousness of the presence of Almighty God in your heart, you *will* fear Him, revere Him and be in constant awe of Him. The amplification of this verse says that you will be "wholly filled and flooded with God Himself." The word "wholly" means entirely and completely. Your Father wants you to be filled at all times with awareness of His awesome indwelling presence.

The Bible says that God "...by (in consequence of) the [action of His] power that is at work within us, is able to [carry out His purpose and] do superabundantly, far over and above all that we [dare] ask or think [infinitely beyond our highest prayers, desires, thoughts, hopes, or dreams]" (Ephesians 3:20)

If you are in the center of God's plan for your life, you can be certain that God is fully able to carry out His purpose for your life. (If you are interested in God's specific plan for your life, see our book, *God's Plan for Your Life*. This book is solidly anchored on 241 verses of Scripture.) You are told in Ephesians 3:20 that God is able to "do superabundantly, far over and above all that you dare ask or think."

God is able to answer every prayer. There is no problem that God Who lives in your heart cannot solve (see Matthew 17:20 and 19:26). If every aspect of your life revolves around your continual awareness that the God of the universe makes His home in your heart, you will have continual reverence and awe for Him.

Once again, the Scripture that we are studying in these first two chapters is mind-boggling. If you meditate often on this Scripture, you will have constant reverence and awe for God.

God is with you at all times. You are never alone. You cannot be lonely if you are continually conscious that your loving Father makes His home in your heart. You will never be afraid of anyone or anything if you are absolutely certain that your loving Father is with you at all times. God said, "Have not I commanded you? Be strong, vigorous, and very courageous. Be not afraid, neither be dismayed, for the Lord your God is with you wherever you go." (Joshua 1:9)

These words that God spoke to Joshua when he succeeded Moses as the leader of Israel are God's words to you today. Your Father *commands* you to "be strong, vigorous and very courageous." *Why* would you ever be afraid of anything if you are absolutely certain that Almighty God is with you wherever you go? "…with us is the Lord our God to help us and to fight our battles…." (II Chronicles 32:8)

God never intended for you to attempt to fight difficult battles that you cannot win with your limited human abilities. Your loving Father promises to help you. He is more than willing to fight battles for you to the degree that you know these supernatural promises and that you have absolute faith that He always does exactly what He says He will do. "God is faithful (reliable, trustworthy, and therefore ever true to His promise, and He can be depended on)..." (I Corinthians 1:9)

All of the promises that we are studying in this chapter are totally, completely and absolutely true. If God says something, you can be certain that He *will* do whatever He promises to do. "...we take comfort and are encouraged and confidently and boldly say, The Lord is my Helper; I will not be seized with alarm [I will not fear or dread or be terrified]..." (Hebrews 13:6)

Know that God is your Helper. Know that God lives in your heart and that He is with you at all times. Do not be afraid of anything.

Have absolute faith that God will always help you to do what you cannot do with the limitations of your human strength and abilities. "Be strong, courageous, and firm; fear not nor be in terror before them, for it is the Lord your God Who goes with you; He will not fail you or forsake you." (Deuteronomy 31:6)

These words that Moses spoke to the Israelites many years apply to you today. No matter how formidable any problem that you face may seem, you are instructed to be strong, courageous and unafraid. Your loving Father will never fail you or forsake you. "...He [God] Himself has said, I will not in any way fail you nor give you up nor leave you without support. [I will] not, [I will] not, [I will] not in any degree leave you helpless nor forsake nor let [you] down (relax My hold on you)! [Assuredly not!]" (Hebrews 13:5)

God always emphasizes through repetition. Please note that the words "I will not" are used four times in this verse of Scripture and the amplification. God assures you that He will never let you down. You can depend on your Father to do exactly what He promises to do.

We believe that any Christian who pays the price of carefully studying the Scripture references in the first two chapters of this book will make the quality decision to revere God and to hold Him in constant awe. Chapter 1 was dedicated primarily to the supernatural power of God. Chapter 2 is dedicated primarily to the fact that the God Who created everything in the universe lives in your heart and that He will help you.

We have established a solid foundation pertaining to the supernatural might and power of God. We now are ready to study additional Scripture that will help you to live in constant reverence and awe for God.

The next chapter explains that God created you to fear Him and revere Him. You will see that God instructs every person on earth to fear Him and to revere Him continually. As we move forward with the Scripture in this chapter, we believe that your reverence and awe for God will increase steadily.

Chapter 3

God Created You to Fear, Revere and Worship Him

The first two chapters contain many scriptural truths pertaining to reverent awe of God. In this chapter we will study Scripture that will explain that God is worthy of reverent awe from every person on earth. "Worthy are You, our Lord and God, to receive the glory and the honor and dominion, for You created all things; by Your will they were [brought into being] and were created." (Revelation 4:11)

We cannot give God enough glory and honor for all that He is and for everyone and everything He has created. "Who shall not reverence and glorify Your name, O Lord [giving You honor and praise in worship]? For You only are holy. All the nations shall come and pay homage and adoration to You, for Your just judgments (Your righteous sentences and deeds) have been made known and displayed." (Revelation 15:4)

This verse begins with a question. Is there anyone who should not reverence and glorify God and give Him honor, praise and worship? God is holy. *Every* person on earth is instructed to pour out adoration to his or her Creator for Who He is and for the great deeds that He has done. "The Lord reigns, let the peoples tremble [with reverential fear]! He sits [enthroned] above the cherubim, let the earth quake!" (Psalm 99:1)

God reigns over the entire universe. People in the world are instructed to tremble before God with reverential fear. If you can even begin to comprehend the magnificence of God, you will be in absolute awe of Him. You will tremble in your awareness of His might, His power and His holiness. "Who is like You, O Lord, among the gods? Who is like You, glorious in holiness, awesome in splendor, doing wonders?" (Exodus 15:11)

God is majestic. He is glorious in His holiness. He is awesome in His splendor. God does great and mighty things that are beyond the limitations of human understanding.

There is no question that God is worthy of our awe. "None at all is like You, O Lord; You are great, and Your name is great in might. Who would not fear You, O King of the nations? For it is fitting to You and Your due! For among all the wise [men or gods] of the nations and in all their kingdoms, there is none like You." (Jeremiah 10:6-7)

Once again the holy Scriptures explain that nothing can compare to God Who is great and mighty and powerful. God is the King of all nations. You will fear and revere God if you truly understand Who He is and the many magnificent things that He has done.

The Bible explains in Exodus 14 how Pharaoh and his mighty Egyptian army were pursuing Moses and the Israelites. Moses and his followers faced a seemingly impossible situation. The deep Red Sea was ahead of them, high mountains were to the right and left and the Egyptian army was behind them.

How did Moses react to this situation? "…he never flinched but held staunchly to his purpose and endured steadfastly as one who gazed on Him Who is invisible." (Hebrews 11:27)

Moses kept moving forward with absolute faith in God. Instead of focusing on the seemingly unsolvable problems that he and the Israelites faced, Moses "gazed on Him Who is invisible."

God honored his faith. God parted the water in the Red Sea so that the Israelites could pass safely through on dry ground. The water returned to destroy the Egyptian army as they attempted to pass through (see Exodus 14:9-31).

Your Father wants you to trust Him completely when you face a seemingly impossible problem. When God parted the waters of the Red Sea, the Israelites were in absolute awe of what God did. They feared Him. They trusted God. "…Israel saw that great work which the Lord did against the Egyptians, and the people [reverently] feared the Lord and trusted in (relied on, remained steadfast to) the Lord…" (Exodus 14:31)

This story from the Bible applies to your life today. As we study the Bible and see the many great miracles that God has performed, you will see that God is worthy of your reverence and awe.

You were created by God to fear and revere Him and to learn and obey His instructions. "All has been heard; the end of the matter is: Fear God [revere and worship Him, knowing that He is] and keep His commandments, for this is the whole of man [the full, original purpose of his creation, the object of God's providence, the root of character, the foundation of all happiness, the adjustment to all inharmonious circumstances and conditions under the sun] and the whole [duty] for every man." (Ecclesiastes 12:13)

We use this verse of Scripture because the scholars who amplified the Bible saw fit to add such extensive amplification to this one verse. The second amplification explains that God *created you* to fear Him and to obey His instructions. If God created *you* to do something, shouldn't you focus continually on what God created *you* to do?

The amplification in this verse says that fearing God and obeying Him is "the root of character and the foundation of all happiness." If you consistently fear and revere God and obey God's specific instructions, your character will become exactly what God desires. You will live a full, happy and complete life because you will be living the way that God created you to live.

God gave freedom of choice to every person He created. If He did not, we would be robots. If you disobey these specific instructions from God, you will block your loving Father from giving you the wonderful blessings that He very much wants to give you (see I Corinthians 6:12 and 8:9).

God instructs *every* person on earth to fear Him and revere Him. "Let all the earth fear the Lord [revere and worship Him]; let all the inhabitants of the world stand in awe of Him." (Psalm 33:8)

Every person on earth is instructed to fear, revere and worship God. Every person is instructed to stand in awe of God. "O worship the Lord in the beauty of holiness; tremble before and reverently fear Him, all the earth." (Psalm 96:9)

Once again, *every* person on the earth is instructed to reverently fear God. When God repeatedly gives you the same instruction, you can be certain that He is emphasizing what He is telling you. "Tremble and reverently fear before Him, all the earth's peoples..." (I Chronicles 16:30)

We have just studied four verses of Scripture where every person on earth is instructed to reverently fear God. Not only does God instruct every person to revere Him with awe, but He also instructs you to fear Him *continually* throughout every day of your life. "Let not your heart envy sinners, but continue in the reverent and worshipful fear of the Lord all the day long." (Proverbs 23:17)

If you truly fear and revere God, you will not envy unbelievers, their possessions and their success. Your reverent awe for God will continue throughout every day of your life. "Blessed (happy, fortunate, and to be envied) is the man who reverently and worshipfully fears [the Lord] at all times [regardless of circumstances], but he who hardens his heart will fall into calamity." (Proverbs 28:14)

God blesses His children who reverently and worshipfully fear Him, regardless of the circumstances they face. People who have hard hearts and do not obey God's instructions to fear Him will block themselves from receiving God's blessings and eventually face severe adversity. "...in every nation he who venerates and has a reverential fear for God, treating Him with worshipful obedience and living uprightly, is acceptable to Him and sure of being received and welcomed [by Him]." (Acts 10:35)

God is very pleased with every person who has reverential fear for Him and worshipfully obeys His instructions. "The Lord takes pleasure in those who reverently and worshipfully fear Him, in those who hope in His mercy and loving-kindness." (Psalm 147:11)

Do you want to please God? If you do, reverently and worshipfully fear Him. Trust completely in your Father's mercy and loving-kindness.

In this chapter we have studied several verses of Scripture that explain that God is worthy of your reverent awe.

You have learned that God created you to fear and revere Him and to obey His instructions. You have learned that God instructs every person on earth to fear and revere Him continually. You have seen that God is very pleased with each of His children who consistently fear Him with reverent awe.

In the next chapter we will study Scripture that instructs you to revere God's Book of Instructions, the Bible. You will see that God repeatedly instructs you to reverently fear Him and His Word and to continually learn and obey His instructions.

Chapter 4

Do What God Instructs You to Do

In the last chapter we studied Ecclesiastes 12:13. We emphasized that the amplification of this verse says that God's purpose in creating a human being was for this person to fear Him and revere Him. This verse also says that keeping God's commandments is part of the reason why God created each of us.

We also studied Deuteronomy 10:2 where we are told that God requires each of us to reverentially fear Him, to walk in all His ways and to love Him. In this chapter we will continue to study and expand on God's instructions in these two verses of Scripture. We will study what the Bible says about the relationship between fearing God, obeying His instructions and loving Him.

The Bible consistently teaches that there is a definite relationship between reverently fearing God and learning and obeying His instructions. "…he shall keep it with him, and he shall read in it all the days of his life, that he may learn [reverently] to fear the Lord his God, by keeping all the words of this law and these statutes and doing them" (Deuteronomy 17:19)

This verse instructs you to keep God's Word with you so that you can read it every day to learn how to reverently fear God by obeying His instructions. If you are highly motivated as a result of the Scripture that we have studied in the first three chapters of this book, you can read the Scripture in this book often to learn how to fear God.

How do you fear God? You fear God by *doing* what your Father instructs you to do. Moses emphasized this scriptural truth when he spoke to the leaders of the Israelites saying, "Assemble the people—men, women, and children, and the stranger and the sojourner within your towns—that they may hear and learn [reverently] to fear the Lord your God and be watchful to do all the words of this law, and that their children, who have not known it, may hear and learn [reverently] to fear the Lord your God..." (Deuteronomy 31:12-13)

Moses instructed the leaders to assemble the people to learn how to reverently fear God and to do what God instructs them to do in His Word. He said they should teach their children to reverently fear God. If you truly desire to reverently fear God, there is no question that God wants you to consistently study and obey His Word. Be like the psalmist David who said, "Teach me Your way, O Lord, that I may walk and live in Your truth; direct and unite my heart [solely, reverently] to fear and honor Your name." (Psalm 86:11)

If you desire to consistently live in reverent awe of God, you will learn God's specific instructions that tell you how to reverently fear Him and to honor His name. Moses taught the Israelites the importance of obeying God's instructions and reverently fearing Him when he said, "Know also in your [minds and] hearts that, as a man disciplines and instructs his son, so the Lord your God disciplines and instructs you. So you shall keep the commandments of the Lord your

God, to walk in His ways and [reverently] fear Him." (Deuteronomy 8:5-6)

There is no question that God instructs you to obey His instructions and to reverently fear Him. So far in this chapter we have studied five passages of Scripture to add to our summary of Ecclesiastes 12:13 and Deuteronomy 10:12-13 in the last chapter. We now have studied *seven* places in the Bible that combine God's instructions to reverently fear Him with learning and obeying His instructions.

These seven verses of Scripture all are from the Old Testament. The New Testament contains similar instructions. Jesus Christ said, "If you know these things, blessed and happy and to be envied are you if you practice them [if you act accordingly and really do them]." (John 13:17)

You need to do more than just know what God instructs you to do. Your Father will bless you when you do what He instructs you to do. The holy Scriptures also say, "…he who looks carefully into the faultless law, the [law] of liberty, and is faithful to it and perseveres in looking into it, being not a heedless listener who forgets but an active doer [who obeys], he shall be blessed in his doing (his life of obedience)." (James 1:25)

This verse and the amplification refer to the Bible as "the law of liberty." The Bible will *set you free* from anything that is blocking you from receiving God's blessings if you look carefully into it every day and if you consistently obey God's instructions.

This verse refers to "a heedless listener who forgets." I believe that God is speaking here of people who hear a sermon in church, but soon forget completely what their pastor taught them. You should attend church regularly and learn from preachers and teachers. However, if you desire to obey

God's instructions to reverently fear Him, you need to study God's Word yourself in *addition* to what you hear in church.

Once again you are instructed to do what God instructs you to do. Your Father again promises that He will bless you abundantly if you consistently learn and obey His instructions. "...we receive from Him whatever we ask, because we [watchfully] obey His orders [observe His suggestions and injunctions, follow His plan for us] and [habitually] practice what is pleasing to Him." (I John 3:22)

This verse of Scripture explains the relationship between answered prayer and faithfully learning and obeying God's instructions. Since we are studying reverent fear and awe of God in this book, we will apply the instruction in this verse to reverently fearing God.

The words "whatever we ask" definitely include reverent fear of God. If you have a deep desire to live in reverent fear of God, pray to your Father. Ask Him to continually show you how to live a life of reverent awe for Him. Make the quality decision to study the Scripture in this book and to do what God instructs you to do to reverently fear Him.

The first amplification in I John 3:22 instructs you to "watchfully" obey God's instructions. Since we are applying this verse to reverent fear of God, you can conclude that God will be very pleased if you study the Scripture we are sharing with you and then do what He instructs you to do. "...No good thing will He withhold from those who walk uprightly." (Psalm 84:11)

When you walk uprightly, you *obey* God's instructions. If you faithfully study and obey God's instructions in regard to reverently fearing Him, or in any other area, your Father will not withhold any good thing from you. He will bless you abundantly. "Take firm hold of instruction, do not let go; guard her, for she is your life." (Proverbs 4:13)

Do not take God's instructions lightly. Hold tightly onto God's instructions in regard to reverently fearing Him. Your life will be transformed if you are determined to consistently learn and obey these scriptural instructions pertaining to reverent fear and awe of God.

In the last chapter we briefly mentioned that God gave you freedom of choice when He created you. *You decide* whether you will pay the price of studying and consistently obeying God's instructions in regard to reverently fearing Him. Do not block God from blessing you by focusing your life on the achievement of personal goals instead of committing to learn and obey God's instructions to fear Him. "...be careful that this power of choice (this permission and liberty to do as you please) which is yours, does not [somehow] become a hindrance (cause of stumbling) to the weak or overscrupulous [giving them an impulse to sin]." (I Corinthians 8:9)

God chose to give each person complete freedom of choice. Do not use the freedom of choice that God gave you to place the pursuit of personal goals ahead of consistently learning how to live in reverent fear and awe of God. Your Father will abundantly bless all of His children who live in reverent fear and awe toward Him.

This chapter is filled with Scripture pertaining to the relationship between fearing God and obeying His instructions. In the next chapter we will study additional Scripture about the relationship between learning and obeying God's instructions and learning how to reverently fear God.

Chapter 5

Show God That You Love Him

Many Christians know little or nothing about what the Bible says in regard to reverent fear of God. Other Christians know some Scripture pertaining to this very important topic, but they are not totally committed to learn and obey God's specific instructions in regard to fearing and revering Him. The psalmist said, "Streams of water run down my eyes, because men do not keep Your law [they hear it not, nor receive it, love it, or obey it]." (Psalm 119:136)

The psalmist, writing under the anointing of God, said that he cried about people who do not love, receive and obey God's instructions. In this book we are specifically referring to God's instructions regarding reverently fearing Him.

God will not punish you if you do not learn and obey these specific instructions. You will punish yourself because you will block your loving Father from giving you the many blessings that He yearns to give to every one of His children who have deep and reverent awe for Him.

Will you pay the price of learning and obeying God's instructions in regard to reverently fearing Him? God said, "Oh, that you had hearkened to My commandments! Then your peace and prosperity would have been like a flowing river, and your righteousness [the holiness and purity of the nation] like the [abundant] waves of the sea." (Isaiah 48:18)

Your Father has a deep desire for you to learn and obey His instructions. In this book we are discussing reverent fear of God so we will apply this verse to obeying God's instructions in this area. If you consistently obey God's instructions in regard to fearing Him and revering Him, peace and prosperity will flow to you. You will become much more pure and holy as a result of consistently turning away from preoccupation with the things of the world to focus on God's instructions to reverently fear Him.

We now would like to give you a two-question quiz. Do you love God? If so, *do you know* what the Bible instructs you to do to show your love for God?

All Christians will answer the first question affirmatively. We have found over the years that many Christians do not know what the Bible instructs us to do to show our love for God. "…the [true] love of God is this: that we do His commands [keep His ordinances and are mindful of His precepts and teaching]. And these orders of His are not irksome (burdensome, oppressive, or grievous)." (I John 5:3)

If you truly love God, you will consistently obey His instructions. The amplification in the last sentence of this verse says that God's instructions are not "irksome, burdensome, oppressive, or grievous." Some people might think that doing what the Bible instructs them to do will make their lives more difficult. Just the opposite is true.

Do you love God? Do you want to learn everything that you can about reverent fear and awe of God? If you do, pay the price to learn and obey God's instructions in regard to reverently fearing Him. Jesus Christ said, "Anyone who does not [really] love Me does not observe and obey My teaching. And the teaching which you hear and heed is not Mine, but [comes] from the Father Who sent Me." (John 14:24)

Jesus said that you do not love Him if you do not obey His teaching. Jesus emphasized that the words that He taught during His earthly ministry came to Him from God.

Do you really love God? If so, *are you* consistently learning and obeying His instructions? Once again, since we are studying reverent fear and awe of God in this book, we ask if you are faithfully learning and obeying God's instructions in regard to reverently fearing Him.

We have done the work for you. We spent hundreds of hours studying the Bible to learn everything that we could about reverent fear of God. This book is filled with specific instructions from God. Make the quality decision that you *will* show your love for your Father by learning and obeying His instructions. "...be doers of the Word [obey the message], and not merely listeners to it, betraying yourselves [into deception by reasoning contrary to the Truth]." (James 1:22)

You are instructed here to *do* what God instructs you to do instead of just listening to His Word being preached and taught and not obeying His instructions. The last part of this verse and the amplification say that Christians who do not obey God will betray themselves by thinking in a way that is contrary to God's ways.

We want to emphasize that both the Old Testament which is based on Jewish Law and the New Testament which is based on the grace that we receive through Jesus Christ emphasize the importance of obeying God's instructions. "...My thoughts are not your thoughts, neither are your ways My ways, says the Lord. For as the heavens are higher than the earth, so are My ways higher than your ways and My thoughts than your thoughts." (Isaiah 55:8-9)

God's ways are very different from the ways of the world. God's ways are much higher than the ways of human beings. Do not make the mistake of basing your life on the limitations of human logic, reason and understanding. You will block your Father from blessing you if you do. Instead, carefully study God's instructions in regard to reverent fear of God.

Do exactly what God instructs you to do even if these instructions are contrary to worldly logic. "Lean on, trust in, and be confident in the Lord with all your heart and mind and do not rely on your own insight or understanding. In all your ways know, recognize, and acknowledge Him, and He will direct and make straight and plain your paths. Be not wise in your own eyes; reverently fear and worship the Lord and turn [entirely] away from evil." (Proverbs 3:5-7)

This passage of Scripture instructs you not to rely on the limitations of human insight and understanding. Do not allow Satan and his demons to deceive you to merely hear the Word of God without consistently paying the price of showing your love for your Father by studying and obeying His instructions.

Do not attempt to understand reverent fear of God with the limitations of human logic and understanding. You are instructed to reverently fear and worship God by "turning entirely away from evil." Refuse to allow Satan and his demons to influence you to think and act in a seemingly logical way that does not line up with God's specific instructions.

Make the quality decision that you will consistently study and meditate on the Scripture references in this book pertaining to reverent fear of God. Make the quality decision that you will not be deceived into thinking that is based on the limitations of human logic and understanding. Fill your mind with scriptural instructions pertaining to reverent fear of God. Show your love for your Father by consistently obeying these specific instructions that He has given to you.

Do you know the most important instruction in the Word of God? Jesus Christ said, "...You shall love the Lord your God with all your heart and with all your soul and with all your mind (intellect). This is the great (most important, principal) and first commandment." (Matthew 22:37-38)

Jesus explains that the most important thing that you will do throughout your life is to love God with *all* your heart, with *all* your soul and with *all* your mind. You have seen that you show your love for God by obeying His instructions.

Children show their love for their parents by obeying their instructions. This same principle applies to showing your love for your heavenly Father by learning and obeying His instructions.

Since we are studying the topic of reverent awe for God, we will look at what Jesus said in this passage of Scripture in relation to this topic. Make the quality decision to show your reverent awe for God by applying your heart, soul and mind to learning and obeying His instructions.

The last two chapters have been devoted to obeying God's instructions. You have seen that you will block your loving Father from blessing you if you disobey His instructions. You have seen that you show your love for God by obeying His instructions.

We are applying the general scriptural instructions in this book to the specific topic of reverent fear and awe of God. In the next chapter we will study Scripture that will explain that your Father wants you to have reverent awe for His Word just as He wants you to have reverent awe for Him.

Chapter 6

Reverent Awe for the Word of God

In this book we are progressively explaining what the Bible says about the fear of God. In Chapter 1 we began by defining the fear of God. We studied several verses of Scripture pertaining to the fear of God. In Chapter 2 we studied Scripture explaining that God lives in your heart if Jesus Christ is your Savior. The same God Who created everyone and everything in the universe lives in your heart. He is with you throughout every minute of every hour of every day of your life.

In Chapter 3 we studied Scripture explaining that God created you to reverently fear Him. God's Word says that everyone should fear Him and that we should fear Him continually. We studied Scripture that explains why God is worthy of your reverent awe and why He is pleased when His children reverently fear Him.

Chapter 4 was devoted entirely to obedience. We studied many verses of Scripture that explain the vital importance of fearing and revering God as He has consistently instructed you to do. In Chapter 5 we studied Scripture explaining that you show your love for God by obeying His instructions.

In the next three chapters we will study what your Father says about having reverence and awe for His Word just as you have reverence and awe for Him. The psalmist prayed that God would show each of us the relationship between His Word and reverently fearing Him. The psalmist said, "Establish Your word and confirm Your promise to Your servant, which is for those who reverently fear and devotedly worship You." (Psalm 119:38)

You *will* have absolute reverence and awe for the Word of God if you are absolutely certain that God *is* the Author of the Bible. "Every Scripture is God-breathed (given by His inspiration) and profitable for instruction, for reproof and conviction of sin, for correction of error and discipline in obedience, [and] for training in righteousness (in holy living, in conformity to God's will in thought, purpose, and action), so that the man of God may be complete and proficient, well fitted and thoroughly equipped for every good work." (II Timothy 3:16-17)

Every word in the Bible is inspired by God. God inspired each of the human authors of the Bible to write every word that they wrote. God gave His supernatural Book of Instructions to His children to show us how He wants us to live. He has shown us how to make whatever corrections we need to make to live the way He wants us to live. (For additional Scripture explaining that God truly is the Author of the Bible, see I Corinthians 2:13, II Corinthians 3:3, Galatians 1:11-12 and I Thessalonians 2:13.)

If you will approach the Word of God each day with certainty that God is the Author, you *will* be in absolute awe of the Bible. God said, "...this is the man to whom I will look and have regard: he who is humble and of a broken or wounded spirit, and who trembles at My word and reveres My commands." (Isaiah 66:2)

Do you want God to approve of how you live? God will bless you if you are humble and teachable, if you tremble at His Word and if you revere His instructions. God instructs you to tremble at His Word just as you would tremble if you suddenly found yourself in His presence. Be like the psalmist who said, "…my heart stands in awe of Your words [dreading violation of them far more than the force of prince or potentate]." (Psalm 119:161)

Are you in awe of the Word of God? Do you hunger and thirst to continually learn more from your Father? The psalmist went on to say, "I rejoice at Your word as one who finds great spoil." (Psalm 119:162)

The word "spoil" in this context means treasure. The Bible is a precious spiritual treasure that your loving Father has given to you. Rejoice at this treasure that you have been given. Nothing in the world can remotely compare to the Bible. "…everything [human] has its limits and end [no matter how extensive, noble, and excellent]; but Your commandment is exceedingly broad and extends without limits [into eternity]." (Psalm 119:96)

Everything on earth that has been created by any human being is temporary. The Word of God is *eternal*. The great truths that you learn from the Word of God have supernatural eternal value that goes far beyond anything in this world. The apostle Peter, writing under the anointing of God, referred to the Bible as, "…the ever living and lasting Word of God." (I Peter 1:23)

As you look at tremendous skyscrapers and other large manmade creations, understand that everything created by man, no matter how great it seems, is temporary. God's supernatural Book of Instructions has great eternal significance. Peter went on to say, "…the Word of the Lord (divine instruction, the Gospel) endures forever…." (I Peter 1:25)

Give the Bible the priority in your life that God instructs you to give to it. The psalmist David said, "…You have exalted above all else Your name and Your word and You have magnified Your word above all Your name!" (Psalm 138:2)

God exalts His name and His Word above everything else. He exalts His Word *above* His name. Give the supernatural Word of God the same priority in your life that God does.

You saw in Isaiah 66:2 at the beginning of this chapter that your Father instructs you to tremble at His Word and to revere His Word. Many Christians do not approach the Bible each day with absolute awe because they are not absolutely certain that God is the Author of the Bible.

If Jesus Christ is your Savior, you have been given the ability to understand the holy Scriptures. Jesus said, "…To you it has been given to know the secrets and mysteries of the kingdom of heaven, but to them it has not been given." (Matthew 13:11)

Jesus Christ became my Savior almost 40 years ago. At that time the business that I had worked so diligently to build was teetering on the verge of bankruptcy. All of the years of labor that I had invested in this business seemed to be lost. However, a man came to me one wonderful day and told me that the problems I faced were not unsolvable. He told me that I would find the solution if I received Jesus Christ as my Savior.

On July 20, 1974, I prayed with this man on the telephone. He was in Oklahoma. I was in New Hampshire. On that day I received Jesus Christ as my Savior.

In my desperation during the months and years before this time, I had studied many positive thinking books. I had filled several three-ring binders with inspirational quotes from the men and women who wrote these books. I had included many verses of Scripture in my three-ring binders even before I received Jesus Christ as my Savior.

I was unable to fully understand this Scripture until I received Jesus as my Savior. Jesus said, "Whoever is of God listens to God. [Those who belong to God hear the words of God.] This is the reason that you do not listen [to those words, to Me]: because you do not belong to God and are not of God or in harmony with Him." (John 8:47)

If Jesus Christ is your Savior, you become a member of the family of God. God *is* your loving Father (see John 1:12-13, Romans 8:15-16, II Corinthians 6:18, Ephesians 2:18-19 and I John 3:1). If you are a member of the family of God, you will be in harmony with God. You will be able to understand His Word.

When Jesus Christ becomes your Savior, the spiritual veil that blocked you from understanding God's Word is removed. "…whenever a person turns [in repentance] to the Lord, the veil is stripped off and taken away." (II Corinthians 3:16)

The man who led me to Christ told me that I would never overcome the problems I faced unless I *saturated* myself in the Word of God. On that day I began to study several Scripture references that I had already collected in my three-ring binders. Suddenly I was able to completely understand this Scripture and how it applied to the problems I faced.

I began to make up 3x5 file cards with verses of Scripture that I knew would help me with the ordeal I faced. I went to a Christian book store and bought books by Christian authors. I searched through these books to find additional Scripture that applied to the problems I faced. I fervently copied this Scripture onto 3x5 file cards.

I soon had a large stack of 3x5 cards. I studied this Scripture continually. I saturated myself in this Scripture as the man who led me to Christ had advised me to do. I finally understood that God *is* the Author of the Bible. I knew that I had the answers from God that I needed on these 3x5 cards.

Today the business that I founded 45 years ago is doing well. This business did not go bankrupt. I am now retired from this business but I still stay in close touch with the man who succeeded me and with my son, Mike, who has worked in this business for 30 years.

I am in absolute awe of what God did for me 39 years ago after I immersed myself in His Word every day. I have continued to saturate myself in God's Word. I have written or co-authored with Judy 27 Christian books and 10 sets of Scripture Meditation Cards. At the age of 82 I have written one or more drafts of ten additional books to be completed during the next five years.

We give away our books and Scripture cards to inmates in prisons and jails and to pastors in Third World countries who preach and teach in their churches from the scriptural contents of these books. Our publications have helped people all over the world. As this book is written, we have received comments from people in *61 countries* who have been helped by our books and Scripture cards.

For the last 39 years, I have had the same attitude toward the Word of God that the apostle Paul had when he said, "...I endorse and delight in the Law of God in my inmost self [with my new nature]." (Romans 7:22)

The words "my new nature" in the amplification of this verse refer to Jesus Christ being my Savior. I have *delighted* in the Word of God ever since the day that Jesus became my Savior. At the age of 82 I still immerse myself in God's Word every day. I am in awe of the Word of God just as I am in awe of God. I cannot get enough of God's supernatural living Word.

God has instructed us to hunger and thirst for His Word. "Like newborn babies you should crave (thirst for, earnestly desire) the pure (unadulterated) spiritual milk, that by it you may be nurtured and grow unto [completed] salvation" (I Peter 2:2)

You can only grow and mature in the spiritual realm to the degree that you hunger and thirst for the Word of God and immerse yourself each day in God's supernatural Book of Instructions. Your Father wants you to have the same attitude toward His Word that the psalmist had when he prayed to God saying, "Open my eyes, that I may behold wondrous things out of Your law. I am a stranger and a temporary resident on the earth; hide not Your commandments from me." (Psalm 119:18-19)

Pray continually asking God to reveal great spiritual truths to you from His Word. If Jesus Christ is your Savior, this world is not your home (see Philippians 3:20 and I Peter 2:11). Turn away from the temporary things of the world to immerse yourself each day in the supernatural eternal Word of God. The psalmist David said, "The law of the Lord is perfect, restoring the [whole] person; the testimony of the Lord is sure, making wise the simple. The precepts of the Lord are right, rejoicing the heart; the commandment of the Lord is pure and bright, enlightening the eyes." (Psalm 19:7-8)

The Word of God is perfect. You will receive supernatural wisdom from God if you consistently study and meditate on His Word. Your heart will sing with joy every day because you will be certain that you are hearing from God. "The [reverent] fear of the Lord is clean, enduring forever; the ordinances of the Lord are true and righteous altogether. More to be desired are they than gold, even than much fine gold; they are sweeter also than honey and drippings from the honeycomb. Moreover, by them is Your servant warned (reminded, illuminated, and instructed); and in keeping them there is great reward." (Psalm 19:9-11)

This passage of Scripture compares reverent fear of God with the reverent awe that your Father wants you to have for His supernatural Word. The Word of God is much more desirable than gold or silver or anything else in the world. Your Father will reward you abundantly if you consistently immerse yourself in the holy Scriptures and if you do what He instructs you to do.

Chapter 7

Effective Bible Study
and Scripture Meditation

In the last chapter we referred several times to Isaiah 66:2 where you are told that God is looking for people who tremble before His Word with the same reverence that they have for God Himself. Isaiah 66:2 instructs you to be "humble and of a broken or wounded spirit."

Some Christians live their lives based on their personal opinions of what life is all about. If you approach reverent awe of God or any other topic in the Bible with the humble desire to learn and to do exactly what God instructs you to do in this area, you have a humble and teachable spirit. "...knowledge is easy to him who [being teachable] understands." (Proverbs 14:6)

If you approach God's Word each day with reverent awe and a humble desire to learn from God, you are humble and you will understand God's Word. The following words that Jesus Christ spoke to a group of Pharisees more than 2,000 years ago apply to each of us today. Jesus said, "...for the sake of your tradition (the rules handed down by your forefathers), you have set aside the Word of God [depriving it of force and authority and making it of no effect]." (Matthew 15:6)

The more that you study the Word of God with a humble and teachable attitude, the more you will turn away from traditional worldly ways of thinking. Some people block the supernatural power of God's Word and make it ineffective in their lives because they think traditionally based on worldly concepts that have been handed down from generation to generation. If you are humble and teachable and you revere the Word of God, you will "...no longer live as the heathen (the Gentiles) do in their perverseness [in the folly, vanity, and emptiness of their souls and the futility] of their minds.." (Ephesians 4:17)

These words that Paul wrote to the Ephesians many years ago apply to your life today. Turn away from the way that unbelievers and Christians who do not revere the Word of God live. Do not allow yourself to live your life in conformity to the folly, emptiness and futility of the ways of the world. The following words that King Solomon spoke to his son are God's words to you today. "Hear, my son, and be wise, and direct your mind in the way [of the Lord]." (Proverbs 23:19)

If you are wise, you will turn away from the world and "direct your mind in the way of the Lord." If you have reverent awe for the Word of God, you will obey the following specific instructions from God. "Do not be conformed to this world (this age), [fashioned after and adapted to its external, superficial customs], but be transformed (changed) by the [entire] renewal of your mind [by its new ideals and its new attitude], so that you may prove [for yourselves] what is the good and acceptable and perfect will of God, even the thing which is good and acceptable and perfect [in His sight for you]." (Romans 12:2)

The amplification in this verse speaks of the "external, superficial customs of the world." If you have absolute reverence and awe for the Word of God, your life will be *transformed* if you renew your mind in the Word of God each day. God will reveal supernatural truths to you that will show you how He wants you to live your life. "...our old (unrenewed) self was nailed to the cross with Him..." (Romans 6:6)

If Jesus Christ is your Savior, your old unrenewed self was nailed to the cross with Him. There is no reason for you to continue thinking the way that you thought before you were saved. Turn completely away from the world's way of doing things by obeying God's instructions to consistently renew your mind by studying His Word. "...you have stripped off the old (unregenerate) self with its evil practices, and have clothed yourselves with the new [spiritual self], which is [ever in the process of being] renewed and remolded into [fuller and more perfect knowledge upon] knowledge after the image (the likeness) of Him Who created it." (Colossians 3:9-10)

Strip off layer after layer of the way that you used to think before Jesus Christ became your Savior. Approach God's Word each day with reverent awe. Allow your Father to remold you to become more and more like He is. "Strip yourselves of your former nature [put off and discard your old unrenewed self] which characterized your previous manner of life and becomes corrupt through lusts and desires that spring from delusion; and be constantly renewed in the spirit of your mind [having a fresh mental and spiritual attitude], and put on the new nature (the regenerate self) created in God's image, [Godlike] in true righteousness and holiness." (Ephesians 4:22-24)

Once again you are instructed to "strip" off the way that you used to think before Jesus Christ became your Savior as you "constantly" renew your mind in God's Word. The amplification in verse 23 says that you will have a "fresh mental and spiritual attitude" if you consistently renew your mind in the Word of God.

If you renew your mind by studying God's Word each day, you will put on the new nature that was created in God's image when Jesus Christ became your Savior. "Study and be eager and do your utmost to present yourself to God approved (tested by trial), a workman who has no cause to be ashamed, correctly analyzing and accurately dividing [rightly handling and skillfully teaching] the Word of Truth." (II Timothy 2:15)

Your Father instructs you to be *eager* to present yourself to Him with the great new spiritual truths that you are learning from His Word. You are instructed to be "a workman who has no cause to be ashamed." In this book we believe that we have taught you from God's Word by "correctly analyzing and accurately dividing" the holy Scriptures in regard to what God teaches about reverent awe of Him.

I would like to stop here to briefly discuss how I study the Word of God. There is no one way to study God's Word. I will share the way that I have studied the holy Scriptures during the past 39 years. This method has helped many people all over the world. Once again, we have received comments from people in 61 countries who have been helped by our books and Scripture cards.

In this book we are studying the Bible in regard to reverent awe of God. When you read this book, we recommend that you highlight or underline key words in each verse of Scripture that are meaningful to you. Write notes in the margins at the side, top or bottom of whatever page you are reading about what you are learning.

I have used the topical method of studying the Bible for 39 years. I decide whatever topic I want to study. I then find every Scripture reference that I can on this topic. I weave them together. This is what we have done with the topic of reverent awe for God in this book. If you will look at the list of books and Scripture Meditation Cards on the first page of this book, you will see that our publications explain many topics.

Every one of our books contains more than 200 verses of Scripture. We have done the work for you. We have spent many hours finding Scripture on the topic of each book and set of Scripture cards. Each set of our Scripture Meditation Cards contains 52 cards. Each set contains approximately 80 verses of Scripture because many cards contain more than two or more verses. I have recorded a CD to accompany each set of Scripture cards.

If you would like to take advantage of the topical method of Bible study that I have used, you can study and meditate in the future on Scripture pertaining to many different topics in addition to the topic of reverent awe for God that we studying in this book. You can follow the example of early Christians who were very eager to learn everything they could about the ways of God. The apostle Paul said that these converts had an "…inclination of mind and eagerness, searching and examining the Scriptures daily to see if these things were so." (Acts 17:11)

Eagerly study the holy Scriptures each day. Learn the great scriptural truths that your Father has made available to every one of His children. At the age of 82, I am still learning new scriptural truths each day. Nothing in my life is more exciting than my daily Bible study.

Now that we have commented on the subject of Bible study, we are ready to discuss the subject of Scripture meditation. We use the following verse of Scripture in almost every one of our books. "This Book of the Law shall not depart out of your mouth, but you shall meditate on it day and night, that you may observe and do according to all that is written in it. For then you shall make your way prosperous, and then you shall deal wisely and have good success." (Joshua 1:8)

God spoke these words directly to Joshua when he succeeded Moses as the leader of Israel. Joshua was approximately 30 years old at that time. He had assisted Moses as a captain in Israel's army. Joshua must have been overwhelmed at the immensity of the challenge of leading Israel at such a young age. God assured Joshua that He would be with him at all times, just as He was with Moses (see Joshua 1:5).

God gave Joshua the specific instructions that we read in Joshua 1:8. This verse refers to the Book of the Law, the first five books of the Old Testament. We have much more Scripture to meditate on today than Joshua had. The Bible today consists of 66 books – 42 in the Old Testament and 26 in the New Testament.

I can tell you from personal experience that, after 39 years of intensive Bible study and Scripture meditation, I am not even scratching the surface of the enormous amount of scriptural truth that is contained in the Bible. The Bible is infinite and eternal. The more that I study and meditate on the holy Scriptures, the more there is for study and meditation.

We now will carefully study Joshua 1:8. I always explain the last part of this verse first. This part of Joshua 1:8 explains God's promises to you if you obey the instructions in the first part of the verse.

First, God promises that you will prosper. The Hebrew word "talasch" that is translated as "prosperous" here means much more than financial prosperity. This word means "to push forward, break out and go over." If you obey God's specific instructions in the first part of Joshua 1:8, you not only will prosper financially but you will be able to break *through* and go *over* obstacles that you face.

This verse goes on to speak of dealing wisely. We will defer our explanation of God's wisdom until Chapters 9 and 10. These two chapters are devoted to the relationship between reverent fear of God and receiving wisdom from God. Part of receiving God's wisdom is to faithfully obey His instructions to meditate day and night on His Word.

The final blessing that God promises is success. We have explained that the Bible contains 66 Books. Out of the tens of thousands of words in the Bible, the word "success" is only used *one time* – in Joshua 1:8 (from *Strong's Exhaustive Concordance of the Bible* that is based on the King James Version). If you want to be successful from God's perspective, you will obey the specific instructions that God gives you in the first part of Joshua 1:8.

Now we will look at God's instructions in the first part of Joshua 1:8. God says that His Word should not depart out of your mouth (because you are meditating on it day and night). The Hebrew word "hagah" that is translated as "meditate" means "to ponder, mutter, speak, study, talk and utter." When you meditate day and night on the Word of God, you *speak* God's Word continually. The Word of God flows out of your mouth every day and night as you meditate on the holy Scriptures with reverent awe.

The final instruction that God gives in Joshua 1:8 is to "observe and do" everything that God's Word instructs you to do. In this book we are studying the topic of reverent awe of God. The more that you meditate on the Scripture in this book, the more you will learn and do what God instructs you to do in regard to living in reverent awe for Him.

We will not give a detailed explanation of Scripture meditation here because we want to focus on the topic of reverent awe of God. Several of our other books explain in detail how to meditate on the Word of God.

When you meditate on a passage of Scripture, you *personalize* the Scripture that you have chosen. You constantly *speak* in the first person the instruction or promise that you have selected. Be like the psalmist who said, "I will meditate on Your precepts and have respect to Your ways [the paths of life marked out by Your law]. I will delight myself in Your statutes; I will not forget Your word." (Psalm 119:15-16)

Do you have great respect for how God instructs you to live? If you do, you will meditate day and night on the holy Scriptures. You will have great *delight* in the Word of God. You will not be able to get enough of God's supernatural Word. You will hunger and thirst to continually learn more from the Creator of the universe Who is the Author of the Bible.

In this chapter we have studied several verses of Scripture pertaining to effective Bible study and Scripture meditation. In the next chapter we will study several additional verses of Scripture that will help *you* to live in reverent awe of God.

Chapter 8

Fill Your Heart with the Word of God

When you study the Word of God, you renew your *mind*. When you meditate day and night on God's Word, the Scripture that you are meditating on drops from your mind down into your *heart*. This chapter will be devoted primarily to what the Bible says about filling your heart with the Word of God.

When the Bible speaks of your heart, it does not refer to the organ in your body that pumps blood. It refers to your spiritual heart. Deep down inside of yourself is a spiritual person who is the real you. When Jesus Christ becomes your Savior, a new spiritual person is born. The Bible refers to this new person as "...the hidden person of the heart..." (I Peter 3:4)

The world focuses primarily on external appearances. God looks at your heart. "...the Lord sees not as man sees; for man looks on the outward appearance, but the Lord looks on the heart." (I Samuel 16:7)

When we studied Romans 12:2 in regard to renewing your mind, the words "external, superficial customs" in the amplification of this verse refer to the ways of the world. When you fill your heart with the Word of God, you are filling your heart with supernatural instructions and promises from the Book that has God as its Author.

In his letter to the Colossians the apostle Paul explained where the home of the Word of God is meant to be. Paul said, "Let the word [spoken by] Christ (the Messiah) have its home [in your hearts and minds] and dwell in you in [all its] richness..." (Colossians 3:16)

The words spoken by Jesus Christ and everything else in the Bible has a spiritual home. If you consistently meditate on the Word of God, your heart is filled with the holy Scriptures. Your life is determined by whatever you truly believe in your heart. "...as he thinks in his heart, so is he...." (Proverbs 23:7)

Whenever you face severe adversity, you will always react based on whatever you deeply believe in your heart. When you consistently meditate on the Word of God, you are programming your heart in a way that is similar to the way that a computer is programmed. You are experiencing God Himself through His Word.

If you truly have reverent awe for the Word of God, you will constantly fill your heart with supernatural instructions and promises from God. As you meditate day and night on the holy Scriptures, the following words that King Solomon spoke to his son are God's instructions to you. "My son, attend to my words; consent and submit to my sayings. Let them not depart from your sight; keep them in the center of your heart." (Proverbs 4:20-21)

Your Father wants you to pay close attention to His Word. You learned in Chapters 4 and 5 the vital importance of obeying God's instructions. The words "not depart from your sight" refer to meditating day and night on the Word of God. If you obey God's instructions to meditate day and night on His Word, you will fill your heart with His Word.

How do you meditate day and night on the Word of God? When I became a Christian 39 years ago, I faced very severe business financial problems. I did not know anything about Scripture meditation. I wrote verses of Scripture that were important to me on 3x5 cards. I carried these cards with me everywhere. Although I did not understand the principles of meditation, that is exactly what I was doing.

I can remember meditating on these cards many times while I was driving my car. I had some of these cards taped to the walls in our home in New Hampshire. I had several of them taped to the bathroom mirror. I had some of these 3x5 cards under a piece of plastic on my office desk. I was exposed to the Scripture references that were important to me throughout every day and night. As I meditated continually on this Scripture, I filled my heart with the supernatural Word of God. "Wise men store up knowledge [in mind and heart]…" (Proverbs 10:14)

The words "store up" in this verse are very important. In the world people attempt to obtain security by storing up money. Security from God's perspective comes from storing up His Word in your mind and your heart. "…you shall lay up these My words in your [minds and] hearts and in your [entire] being…" (Deuteronomy 11:18)

God emphasizes through repetition. The words "store up" and "lay up" are similar. There is no question that your Father wants you to store up His Word in your mind and your heart. If you have reverent awe for the Word of God, you will constantly store up Scripture within yourself. "Keep and guard your heart with all vigilance and above all that you guard, for out of it flow the springs of life." (Proverbs 4:23)

You are instructed to "guard your heart with all vigilance." When you guard something, you protect whatever you are guarding. When you guard your heart vigilantly, you are very careful about what you allow to come into your heart. You protect yourself by constantly storing up God's Word in your heart to keep the ways of the world from filling your heart. Your heart is the key to your life.

If you consistently fill your heart by meditating day and night on God's supernatural Word, your faith in God will become deep, strong and unwavering. The Bible refers to itself as being "...effectually at work in you who believe [exercising its superhuman power in those who adhere to and trust in and rely on it]." (I Thessalonians 2:13)

If you consistently fill your heart with the Word of God, the "superhuman power" of God's Word will be released in your life to the degree that you adhere to, trust in and rely on God's instructions and promises. Your heart will sing with joy, regardless of the circumstances you face, because the supernatural power of God's Word in your heart is much greater than any adversity you will face. Jesus Christ said, "...The seed is the Word of God." (Luke 8:11)

God's Word is a spiritual seed. Your heart is spiritual soil. You plant spiritual seeds in your heart when you meditate day and night on Scripture. Jesus said, "...as for that [seed] in the good soil, these are [the people] who, hearing the Word, hold it fast in a just (noble, virtuous) and worthy heart, and steadily bring forth fruit with patience." (Luke 8:15)

If you meditate day and night on God's Word, you are consistently planting spiritual seeds in your heart. If you hold fast to what you are doing and you patiently wait for God to do what He promises to do, you will bring forth fruit steadily.

Filling your heart with God's Word is not something to do occasionally. If you truly revere God and His Word, you will faithfully obey your Father's instructions to study and meditate on His Word every day of your life.

II Corinthians 4:16 instructs you to renew your mind in God's Word "day by day." Ephesians 4:23 tells you to renew your mind in God's Word "constantly." Both Joshua 1:8 and Psalm 1:2-3 instruct you to meditate "day and night" on the Word of God.

You will be able to persevere patiently if the supernatural power of God's Word in your mind and your heart becomes more meaningful to you than the severity of any adversity you face. "...with God nothing is ever impossible and no word from God shall be without power or impossible of fulfillment." (Luke 1:37)

There is no problem that God cannot solve. Trust God completely. Trust the promises in His Word completely. If you consistently fill your heart with the power of God's Word, your faith in God will grow steadily.

You will have a deep inner certainty that the supernatural power of God's Word that fills your heart to overflowing will enable you to overcome any adversity you face. "How shall a young man cleanse his way? By taking heed and keeping watch [on himself] according to Your word [conforming his life to it]." (Psalm 119:9)

You undoubtedly take a bath or shower each day to cleanse your body. You cleanse yourself in the spiritual realm by living in obedience to the Word of God that has been programmed into your mind and your heart by consistent Bible study and Scripture meditation. "...since these [great] promises are ours, beloved, let us cleanse ourselves from everything that contaminates and defiles body and spirit, and bring [our] consecration to completeness in the [reverential] fear of God." (II Corinthians 7:1)

God's great promises are your Father's gift to you. Consistently cleanse yourself in God's Word from "everything that contaminates and defiles body and spirit." If you obey these instructions, you will "bring your consecration to completeness in the reverential fear of God."

The word "consecration" means to set apart as holy. If you consistently study and meditate on God's Word, you will be cleansed from the impurities of the world. You will become more and more reverent in your awe of God.

In the last three chapters we have studied many of God's instructions and promises. You have seen that God instructs you to revere His Word just as you revere Him. If you truly revere the Word of God, you *will* fill your mind and your heart with the holy Scriptures every day.

In the next two chapters we will study Scripture that explains the relationship between reverent awe for the Word of God and receiving supernatural wisdom from God. Nothing in the world can remotely compare with the supernatural wisdom that your Father will give you if you consistently live in reverent awe of Him and His Word.

Chapter 9

Reverent Fear of God
and Wisdom from God

We will begin this chapter by looking at a scriptural definition of God's wisdom. The amplification in *The Amplified Bible* says that wisdom is "comprehensive insight into the ways and purposes of God..." (Colossians 1:28).

We did not look into a dictionary for this definition because we are talking about God's wisdom, not the wisdom of the world. This definition of God's wisdom comes from the scholars who compiled *The Amplified Bible*.

The word "comprehensive" means full understanding. You will have a much better understanding of God's ways and purposes if you study and meditate on the Scripture in this chapter and the next chapter. You will be able to receive supernatural wisdom from God when your human wisdom is completely inadequate to cope with any challenge that you face. "Oh, the depth of the riches and wisdom and knowledge of God! How unfathomable (inscrutable, unsearchable) are His judgments (His decisions)! And how untraceable (mysterious, undiscoverable) are His ways (His methods, His paths)!" (Romans 11:33)

The depth of God's wisdom and knowledge is immeasurable by any human standard. God's ways are unfathomable. The dictionary says that unfathomable means "impossible to understand because of being very mysterious or complicated." We also are told that the wisdom and knowledge of God are inscrutable which means not readily understood.

God's ways are very different and very much higher than the ways of human beings (see Isaiah 55:8-9). If you have reverent awe for God and His Word and you study and meditate on the Scripture in these two chapters, you will receive supernatural wisdom from God.

The following words that King Solomon spoke to his son are your Father's words to you. "My son, if you will receive my words and treasure up my commandments within you, making your ear attentive to skillful and godly Wisdom and inclining and directing your heart and mind to understanding [applying all your powers to the quest for it]; Yes, if you cry out for insight and raise your voice for understanding, if you seek [Wisdom] as for silver and search for skillful and godly Wisdom as for hidden treasures, then you will understand the reverent and worshipful fear of the Lord and find the knowledge of [our omniscient] God." (Proverbs 2:1-5)

This passage of Scripture connects receiving wisdom from God and the fear of God. You are instructed to "treasure up" God's Word within yourself. The Word of God is a supernatural treasure. Continually store up this great treasure in your mind and your heart.

If you obey this instruction, you will be "attentive" to God's wisdom. You will tune in to the wisdom of God. You will understand more and more about the ways and purposes of God. If you consistently seek God's wisdom as the magnificent spiritual treasure that it is, you will understand reverent fear of the Lord. You will be able to obtain supernatural knowledge from omniscient God.

When you fear God, you revere Him. You hold Him in constant awe. Your life is centered around your reverent awe for God. If these words describe you, you will receive supernatural wisdom from God. "…the reverential and worshipful fear of the Lord—that is Wisdom…" (Job 28:28)

Reverential fear of God enables you to receive wisdom from God. The more that you turn toward God and away from the ways of the world, the more you will understand God's ways. "The reverent fear and worship of the Lord is the beginning of Wisdom…" (Psalm 111:10)

Reverent fear of God is the first essential to receiving supernatural wisdom from God. "The reverent and worshipful fear of the Lord is the beginning (the chief and choice part) of Wisdom…" (Proverbs 9:10)

Please note the almost identical wording is Psalm 111:10 and Proverbs 9:10. There is no question that reverent fear of God leads you to the wisdom of God. "The reverent and worshipful fear of the Lord is the beginning and the principal and choice part of knowledge [its starting point and its essence]" (Proverbs 1:7)

So far in this chapter we have studied five passages of Scripture that explain the relationship between reverent fear of God and receiving wisdom and knowledge from God. God always emphasizes through repetition. There is no question that your Father wants you to understand the relationship between reverent awe of Him and receiving supernatural wisdom and knowledge from Him. "The reverent and worshipful fear of the Lord brings instruction in Wisdom…" (Proverbs 15:33)

If you truly have reverent fear for God, your Father will continually teach you great truths about receiving His supernatural wisdom. "…the Spirit of the Lord shall rest upon Him—the Spirit of wisdom and understanding, the Spirit of counsel and might, the Spirit of knowledge and of the reverential and obedient fear of the Lord—and shall make Him of quick understanding, and His delight shall be in the reverential and obedient fear of the Lord. And He shall not judge by the sight of His eyes, neither decide by the hearing of His ears" (Isaiah 11:2-3)

This passage of Scripture is a prophecy pertaining to Jesus Christ. It accurately prophesied that the Holy Spirit would rest upon Jesus throughout His earthly ministry. The Holy Spirit continually gave supernatural wisdom, knowledge and understanding to Jesus. If you consistently learn from the Holy Spirit, you will not make decisions based upon the limitations of human understanding that is centered on what you see with your eyes and hear with your ears.

The Holy Spirit is omnipresent. He lives in the heart of every person who has received Jesus Christ as his or her Savior (see Galatians 4:6). "…God's Spirit has His permanent dwelling in you [to be at home in you, collectively as a church and also individually]…" (I Corinthians 3:16)

The same Holy Spirit Who lived in the heart of Jesus Christ during His earthly ministry makes His permanent home in your heart if Jesus is your Savior. He is with you at all times. He will guide you to the degree that you willingly yield control of your life to Him. "If we live by the [Holy] Spirit, let us also walk by the Spirit. [If by the Holy Spirit we have our life in God, let us go forward walking in line, our conduct controlled by the Spirit.]" (Galatians 5:25)

Please note that the amplification in this verse instructs you to have your conduct controlled by the Holy Spirit. If you truly have reverent awe for God, you will not attempt to control your life with your limited human abilities. You will yield control of your life to the Holy Spirit. You will receive wisdom, knowledge and understanding from God. "…where shall Wisdom be found? And where is the place of understanding? Man knows not the price of it; neither is it found in the land of the living." (Job 28:12-13)

The world knows nothing about the wisdom of God. You can only receive wisdom from God through reverent awe of Him and yielding control of your life to the Holy Spirit. "It cannot be gotten for gold, neither shall silver be weighed for the price of it. It cannot be valued in [terms of] the gold of Ophir, in the precious onyx or beryl, or the sapphire. Gold and glass cannot equal [Wisdom], nor can it be exchanged for jewels or vessels of fine gold. No mention shall be made of coral or of crystal; for the possession of Wisdom is even above rubies or pearls." (Job 28:15-18)

All of the money in the world could not purchase God's supernatural wisdom. *Nothing* that the world offers can remotely compare to receiving wisdom from God. "…skillful and godly Wisdom is better than rubies or pearls, and all the things that may be desired are not to be compared to it." (Proverbs 8:11)

The Word of God instructs you to turn away from focusing on accumulating wealth in excess of your family's needs. "Weary not yourself to be rich; cease from your own [human] wisdom." (Proverbs 23:4)

You will not depend on the limitations of wisdom from any worldly source if you are absolutely certain that you can receive supernatural wisdom from God. "Let no person deceive himself. If anyone among you supposes that he is wise in this age, let him become a fool [let him discard his worldly discernment and recognize himself as dull, stupid, and foolish, without true learning and scholarship], that he may become [really] wise." (I Corinthians 3:18)

You will deceive yourself if you turn to worldly sources looking for wisdom. "…this world's wisdom is foolishness (absurdity and stupidity) with God, for it is written, He lays hold of the wise in their [own] craftiness; and again, The Lord knows the thoughts and reasonings of the [humanly] wise and recognizes how futile they are." (I Corinthians 3:19-20)

Please note the emphatic words in this passage of Scripture and the amplification. God looks at the world's wisdom as "foolishness, absurdity and stupidity." Human wisdom is described as being "futile." "…in much [human] wisdom is much vexation, and he who increases knowledge increases sorrow." (Ecclesiastes 1:18)

This verse says that you will receive "much vexation" if you consistently seek human wisdom. The word "vexation" means distress. The more that you seek wisdom from worldly sources, the more problems you will bring upon yourself. Human wisdom and knowledge are completely insufficient. If you truly fear and revere God, you will receive His supernatural wisdom.

In this chapter we have seen that God's wisdom is comprehensive insight into the ways and purposes of God. We studied several verses of Scripture pertaining to the relationship between reverent fear of God and receiving supernatural wisdom and knowledge from God. You have seen that we cannot even begin to comprehend the magnitude of God's wisdom. We closed the chapter by studying four passages of Scripture that explain the futility of seeking wisdom from worldly sources.

In the next chapter we will look into God's Word for more instructions on the source of wisdom and how to receive

God's wisdom. We also will study Scripture that will explain the tremendous blessings that your Father will give to you if you learn and obey His specific instructions for receiving His supernatural wisdom.

Chapter 10

God Yearns to Give You
His Supernatural Wisdom

We live in a very exciting time. The wisdom of God that once was hidden from human beings now has been revealed to us. "...what we are setting forth is a wisdom of God once hidden [from the human understanding] and now revealed to us by God—[that wisdom] which God devised and decreed before the ages for our glorification [to lift us into the glory of His presence]." (I Corinthians 2:7)

God has provided wisdom for us that is so great that this wisdom can bring us into the glory of His presence. "He hides away sound and godly Wisdom and stores it for the righteous (those who are upright and in right standing with Him)..." (Proverbs 2:7)

There is only one way to be in right standing with God and that is to receive Jesus Christ as your Savior. You can receive supernatural wisdom and knowledge from God if Jesus is your Savior. "...Christ (the Anointed One). In Him all the treasures of [divine] wisdom (comprehensive insight into the ways and purposes of God) and [all the riches of spiritual] knowledge and enlightenment are stored up and lie hidden." (Colossians 2:2-3)

God's wisdom and many other blessings are given to His children who truly are humble. "...God sets Himself against the proud and haughty, but gives grace [continually] to the lowly (those who are humble enough to receive it)." (James 4:6)

Proud people do not revere God because their lives are centered around themselves. Proud people block themselves from receiving God's wisdom and other blessings. God actually sets Himself against people who are proud because they are their own little gods. God continually gives His wisdom and other blessings to His children who are humble enough to receive His grace.

If God truly is in first place in your life and your life revolves around your reverent awe for Him, you definitely are humble. "When swelling and pride come, then emptiness and shame come also, but with the humble (those who are lowly, who have been pruned or chiseled by trial, and renounce self) are skillful and godly Wisdom and soundness." (Proverbs 11:2)

Proud people live empty lives because their lives are centered around themselves. If you truly are humble and you turn away from selfish desires, you are able to receive supernatural wisdom from God.

God promises to give His supernatural wisdom to every one of His children who ask for His wisdom and have deep, strong and unwavering faith that He will give His wisdom to them. "If any of you is deficient in wisdom, let him ask of the giving God [Who gives] to everyone liberally and ungrudgingly, without reproaching or faultfinding, and it will be given him. Only it must be in faith that he asks with no wavering (no hesitating, no doubting). For the one who wavers (hesitates, doubts) is like the billowing surge out at sea that is blown hither and thither and tossed by the wind.

For truly, let not such a person imagine that he will receive anything [he asks for] from the Lord, [for being as he is] a man of two minds (hesitating, dubious, irresolute), [he is] unstable and unreliable and uncertain about everything [he thinks, feels, decides]." (James 1:5-8)

If you need wisdom from God, ask God for His wisdom. Ask your Father with deep, strong and unwavering faith that He will give His supernatural wisdom to you. Do not allow doubt and unbelief to block your Father from giving His wisdom to you as He has promised to do.

We explained in Chapter 6 that, if you revere God, you also will revere His Word. If you love the Word of God, you will be like the psalmist who said, "Oh, how love I Your law! It is my meditation all the day. You, through Your commandments, make me wiser than my enemies, for [Your words] are ever before me. I have better understanding and deeper insight than all my teachers, because Your testimonies are my meditation. I understand more than the aged, because I keep Your precepts [hearing, receiving, loving, and obeying them]." (Psalm 119:97-100)

The psalmist meditated continually on the Word of God. If you also meditate day and night on the holy Scriptures (see Joshua 1:8 and Psalm 1:2-3), you will receive supernatural wisdom from God because God's Word will be at the forefront of your consciousness. The psalmist said that he had better understanding and deeper insight than all of his teachers because he meditated on God's Word. These same blessings are available to you if you faithfully obey your Father's instructions to consistently meditate on His Word and to do what He instructs you to do.

The more that you meditate on the Word of God and obey God's instructions, the more understanding and insight you will receive from your Father. You will be like the psalmist who said, "I have not turned aside from Your ordinances, for You Yourself have taught me. How sweet are Your words to my taste, sweeter than honey to my mouth! Through Your precepts I get understanding; therefore I hate every false way. Your word is a lamp to my feet and a light to my path." (Psalm 119:102-105)

If you fear and revere God and His Word, God Himself will teach you. Your loving Father will give you understanding and enlightenment. The understanding that God gives you will be like a light that shines to show you where God wants you to go. Psalm 119:105 is the verse that gave us the name for Lamplight Ministries. We know from thousands of testimonies from people in more 60 countries that our books and Scripture cards are a lamp and a light in the lives of many people.

If you meditate day and night on God's Word, this meditation will be like turning on a supernatural light from God. Satan will not be able to pull you into spiritual darkness (see Ephesians 5:11 and 6:12-13, Colossians 1:13, I Peter 2:9 and I John 1:5). If you meditate day and night on God's Word, the Word of God will come alive inside of you. You will receive understanding from God that you cannot obtain in any other way.

Every Christian who truly reveres God will meditate day and night on His Word. We studied this topic in Chapter 7. "Hear instruction and be wise, and do not refuse or neglect it. Blessed (happy, fortunate, to be envied) is the man who listens to me, watching daily at my gates, waiting at the posts of my doors. For whoever finds me [Wisdom] finds life and draws forth and obtains favor from the Lord." (Proverbs 8:33-35)

This instruction that King Solomon gave to his son is God's instruction to you. Please note that you are instructed to "watch daily at God's gates." Numerous surveys have shown that many Christians do not obey God's instructions to study His Word each day (see II Corinthians 4:16) and to meditate day and night on the holy Scriptures (see Joshua 1:8).

Your Father will bless you with His wisdom if you consistently study and meditate on His Word. "Happy (blessed, fortunate, enviable) is the man who finds skillful and godly Wisdom, and the man who gets understanding [drawing it forth from God's Word and life's experiences], for the gaining of it is better than the gaining of silver, and the profit of it better than fine gold. Skillful and godly Wisdom is more precious than rubies; and nothing you can wish for is to be compared to her." (Proverbs 3:13-15)

You will receive a tremendous blessing from God if you learn how to receive wisdom and understanding from His Word and from the experiences in your life if you live in obedience to God's instructions. "Get skillful and godly Wisdom, get understanding (discernment, comprehension, and interpretation); do not forget and do not turn back from the words of my mouth. Forsake not [Wisdom], and she will keep, defend, and protect you; love her, and she will guard you." (Proverbs 4:5-6)

Eagerly pursue the wisdom, understanding, discernment and comprehension that your Father has made available to you. Do not turn away from the Word of God. You are told that God's wisdom will keep, defend, protect and guard you if you love God and His wisdom. "...wisdom shields and preserves the life of him who has it." (Ecclesiastes 7:12)

God emphasizes through repetition. Your Father emphasizes that you will receive supernatural protection through His wisdom. "A wise man is strong and is better than a strong man, and a man of knowledge increases and strengthens his power" (Proverbs 24:5)

Supernatural strength is available to you through the wisdom of God. Jesus Christ has provided supernatural strength to every person who has received Him as his or her Savior. "I have strength for all things in Christ Who empowers me [I am ready for anything and equal to anything through Him Who infuses inner strength into me; I am self-sufficient in Christ's sufficiency]." (Philippians 4:13)

You just saw in Proverbs 24:5 that God will strengthen you supernaturally if you are wise. All of the strength that you will ever need for any challenge you will ever face is available to you through Jesus Christ Who lives in your heart if He is your Savior (see Ephesians 3:17).

In this chapter you have seen that the wisdom of God is available to every person who has received Jesus Christ as his or her Savior. You have seen the relationship that exists between daily study and meditation on the Word of God and receiving God's supernatural wisdom. You have learned that your Father bless you abundantly if you learn how to receive His wisdom. In the next chapter we will study Scripture pertaining to wonderful blessings that God gives to His children who center their lives around reverent awe for Him.

Chapter 11

God Blesses His Children Who Revere Him

God promises many blessings to His children who consistently live a life of reverent awe toward Him. We have mentioned some of these blessings in previous chapters. In this chapter we will focus on all of the blessings that your Father will give to you if you reverently fear Him.

Some Christians do not have reverent awe for God. They respect Him, but their lives do not revolve around their reverent awe for Him. Your Father does not want you to merely live a religious life by going to church regularly, praying for a few minutes each day and living a moral life and then living the remainder of your life focusing on worldly goals.

Your Father wants your relationship with Him to be one of reverent awe. In the last two chapters we studied what the Word of God says about the supernatural wisdom, knowledge and understanding that God will pour out on His children who fear Him and revere Him. He said, "Oh, that they had such a [mind and] heart in them always [reverently] to fear Me and keep all My commandments, that it might go well with them and with their children forever!" (Deuteronomy 5:29)

Please note the word "always" in this verse. Your Father wants you to live a life of consistent reverent awe toward Him. He wants you to consistently study, learn and obey the instructions that He has given to you in His Book of Instructions, the Bible. Your life and the lives of your children will be blessed if you consistently fear God and obey His instructions. "…he who [reverently] fears and respects the commandment [of God] is rewarded." (Proverbs 13:13)

Your Father promises to reward you if you revere His Word. If you are absolutely *certain* that God truly is the Author of the Bible (see Psalm 119:129, I Corinthians 2:13, II Corinthians 3:3, Galatians 1:11-12, I Thessalonians 2:13 and II Timothy 3:16), you will have reverence and awe for the holy Scriptures.

We studied Isaiah 66:2 in Chapter 6. In this verse God instructs us to tremble at His Word and to revere His instructions. The psalmist David said, "Oh, how great is Your goodness, which You have laid up for those who fear, revere, and worship You…" (Psalm 31:19)

This verse explains that God stores up great blessings for His children who fear, revere and worship Him. God will bless you abundantly if you consistently turn away from preoccupation with people, places and events in the world to center your life around your reverent awe for Him. "He will bless those who reverently and worshipfully fear the Lord, both small and great." (Psalm 115:13)

God blesses worldly leaders who fear Him. He also blesses His children who fear Him even though they do not have great stature in the world. "Blessed (happy, fortunate, to be envied) is everyone who fears, reveres, and worships the Lord, who walks in His ways and lives according to His commandments." (Psalm 128:1)

Please note the word "everyone" in this verse. God blesses every one of His children who consistently fear, revere and worship Him and obey His instructions. You cannot make a better decision than to live your life in constant reverence and awe of God and to consistently study and obey God's Word.

Fearing God is so important to God that He commanded Moses to teach the Israelites to reverently fear Him. Moses said, "Now this is the instruction, the laws, and the precepts which the Lord your God commanded me to teach you, that you might do them in the land to which you go to possess it, that you may [reverently] fear the Lord your God, you and your son and your son's son, and keep all His statutes and His commandments which I command you all the days of your life, and that your days may be prolonged." (Deuteronomy 6:1-2)

If you reverently fear and obey God and you teach your children to fear and obey God, your Father will give you a long life. Your Father does not want you to die prematurely. He wants you to live a full and meaningful life. The following words that King Solomon spoke to his son are God's words to you. "Hear, O my son, and receive my sayings, and the years of your life shall be many." (Proverbs 4:10)

In Chapters 9 and 10 we studied the supernatural wisdom that God gives to His children who reverently fear Him. If you consistently receive wisdom from God, you will live a long and full life. God said, "For by me [Wisdom from God] your days shall be multiplied, and the years of your life shall be increased." (Proverbs 9:11)

God promises repeatedly to give long life to His children who fear Him and revere Him. "The reverent and worshipful fear of the Lord prolongs one's days, but the years of the wicked shall be made short." (Proverbs 10:27)

I can tell you from personal experience that God's promises pertaining to long life are true. I am 82 years old as I write these words. I fear God and revere Him. Every aspect of my life revolves around God and my deep and constant desire is to serve Him and to help as many people as possible with the anointing that He has given me.

Many retired people devote their lives entirely to the pursuit of pleasure. I cannot imagine being 82 years old and devoting my life entirely to the pursuit of pleasure. I have hobbies that I enjoy. I spend time on these hobbies, but my hobbies come after my writing time each day. My life's work is writing Christian books that are solidly anchored on the Bible.

Judy is eight years younger than I am. Her health is excellent. She attributes a great deal of her good health to studying the Bible throughout her life. At age 21 she began studying health and fitness and applying what she learned. At the age of 74 Judy is filled with vibrant energy. I would not be alive today if I did not follow many of the health recommendations that Judy has given to me (see our website, lamplight.net, for many of Judy's health discoveries.)

Judy and I live in reverent awe of God because we are coming to know Him more intimately each day. The psalmist David said, "Who is the man who reverently fears and worships the Lord? Him shall He teach in the way that he should choose." (Psalm 25:12)

If you live a life of reverent awe toward God, your loving Father will teach you. He will guide you. "…His mercy (His compassion and kindness toward the miserable and afflicted) is on those who fear Him with godly reverence, from generation to generation and age to age." (Luke 1:50)

God is merciful, compassionate and kind to all of His children who reverently fear Him. The psalmist David said,

"For as the heavens are high above the earth, so great are His mercy and loving-kindness toward those who reverently and worshipfully fear Him." (Psalm 103:11)

God always emphasizes through repetition. Just a few verses later, David, writing under the anointing of God, said, "...the mercy and loving-kindness of the Lord are from everlasting to everlasting upon those who reverently and worshipfully fear Him..." (Psalm 103:17)

God will give you mercy and loving-kindness throughout your life if you fear Him with reverent awe. Your Father promises that He will help you and protect you if you fear and revere Him and trust Him completely. "You who [reverently] fear the Lord, trust in and lean on the Lord! He is their Help and their Shield." (Psalm 115:11)

If your relationship with God is filled with reverent awe, you will trust Him and lean on Him. "The Angel of the Lord encamps around those who fear Him [who revere and worship Him with awe] and each of them He delivers." (Psalm 34:7)

Please note the capitalization of the word "Angel" in this verse. Many scholars believe that this word refers to Jesus Christ. In any event, you can be certain that a mighty and powerful Angel of God will protect you if you revere God and worship Him with awe. "In the reverent and worshipful fear of the Lord there is strong confidence, and His children shall always have a place of refuge." (Proverbs 14:26)

If you truly fear God and revere Him, you can be certain that your Father will provide a place of protection for you when you face severe adversity. "The Lord of hosts—regard Him as holy and honor His holy name [by regarding Him as your only hope of safety], and let Him be your fear and let Him be your dread [lest you offend Him by your fear of man and distrust of Him]. And He shall be a sanctuary [a sacred and indestructible asylum to those who reverently fear and trust in Him]..." (Isaiah 8:13-14)

Please note the words "your only hope of safety" in the amplification of verse 13. If you fear God, you can trust Him completely to protect you. Do not place your faith primarily in worldly sources of security. If you truly fear and revere God, you can be certain that your Father will keep you safe. "The reverent, worshipful fear of the Lord leads to life, and he who has it rests satisfied; he cannot be visited with [actual] evil." (Proverbs 19:23)

If you live in constant reverence and awe toward God, you will live a full and complete life. Satan and his demons will not be able to influence you. "...the Light shines on in the darkness, for the darkness has never overpowered it [put it out or absorbed it or appropriated it, and is unreceptive to it]." (John 1:5)

Please note the capitalization of the word "Light" in this verse. This word refers to the Light of God. When the Bible speaks of darkness, it refers to Satan. If you truly fear and revere God, the Light of God will always overpower the darkness of Satan. "...by the reverent, worshipful fear of the Lord men depart from and avoid evil." (Proverbs 16:6)

Both John 1:5 and Proverbs 16:6 indicate that Satan cannot influence you if you live a life of constant reverent awe of God. "He will fulfill the desires of those who reverently and worshipfully fear Him..." (Psalm 145:19)

This verse refers to the fulfillment that you will experience if you reverently fear God. If you fear God and revere Him, your desires and God's desires for your life will be the same. "O fear the Lord, you His saints [revere and worship Him]! For there is no want to those who truly revere and worship Him with godly fear." (Psalm 34:9)

Please note the words "no want" in this verse. Your Father will supernaturally meet all of your needs if you consistently live in reverent awe of Him. If you truly fear God and revere Him, you will not turn to the world for your needs. God will provide everything that you will ever need. "...they who seek (inquire of and require) the Lord [by right of their need and on the authority of His Word], none of them shall lack any beneficial thing." (Psalm 34:10)

This chapter is filled with many blessings that God promises to give to His children who reverently fear Him and obey His instructions. In the next chapter we will study Scripture pertaining to living a life of total commitment to God. You will live a committed life if you have reverent awe for God.

Chapter 12

Total Commitment to God

In the first 11 chapters of this book we have studied many verses of Scripture pertaining to reverent awe of God. We have explained the scriptural instructions that tell you how to live in reverent fear of God. The remainder of this book will contain many additional scriptural instructions that will explain exactly what to do to live in reverent awe of God.

The following passage of Scripture gives specific instructions that explain what your Father instructs you to do to live in reverent awe of Him. "…what does the Lord your God require of you but [reverently] to fear the Lord your God, [that is] to walk in all His ways, and to love Him, and to serve the Lord your God with all your [mind and] heart and with your entire being, to keep the commandments of the Lord and His statutes which I command you today for your good?" (Deuteronomy 10:12-13)

If you sincerely desire to live in reverent awe of God, you are instructed to "walk in His ways" – to consistently do your best to learn and obey His instructions in the Bible. You are instructed to love God. In Chapter 5 we studied Scripture explaining that you show your love for God by obeying Him.

You are instructed to "serve the Lord your God with all your mind and heart and with your entire being." God has a specific plan for the life of each person (see Psalm 139:16, Jeremiah 1:5 and Ephesians 2:10). If you are interested in obeying these instructions from God, we recommend our book, *God's Plan for Your Life.* This book is solidly anchored on 241 verses of Scripture with a simple and easy-to-understand explanation of each passage of Scripture.

Reverent awe of God requires *total commitment* to God. Many Christians are not totally committed to God. To these people God is a God of Sunday mornings and possibly one other church service a week, a few minutes of prayer each day and possibly some Bible study. Several surveys have shown that many Christians do not study the Bible. They depend completely on their pastor to do their Bible study for them.

Many Christians live the marginal Christian lifestyle that we have just described. The remainder of their lives is focused on themselves, their families, their vocation, accumulating wealth and/or various interests and hobbies. Your Father wants every aspect of your life to revolve around Him. You cannot reverently fear God if you allow anyone or anything to come ahead of Him. When you revere God, He always is at the center of your life.

If you truly fear God, you will humble yourself before Him. You will consistently turn away from personal goals with a deep and sincere desire to draw closer to God, to live in complete obedience to His instructions and to revere Him at all times. You will turn away from a surface relationship with God to the deeper and more meaningful relationship that is required to revere Him.

If Jesus Christ is your Savior, God has forgiven your sins. You will live throughout eternity with Him in the glory of heaven. God also forgave your sins so that you will fear Him and revere Him during the remainder of your life on earth. "...there is forgiveness with You [just what man needs], that You may be reverently feared and worshiped." (Psalm 130:4)

God gives you forgiveness so that you will reverently fear Him and worship Him. "...work out (cultivate, carry out to the goal, and fully complete) your own salvation with reverence and awe and trembling (self-distrust, with serious caution, tenderness of conscience, watchfulness against temptation, timidly shrinking from whatever might offend God and discredit the name of Christ)." (Philippians 2:12)

What does God instruct you to do to work out and fully complete your salvation? He instructs you to complete your salvation with "reverence and awe and trembling." The amplification in this verse explains that you live this way by turning away from trusting in yourself and continually doing your best to live in a way that will not "offend God and discredit the name of Christ."

Some Christians do not have a close and intimate relationship with God because they do not have reverential awe for Him. God said, "...this people draw near Me with their mouth and honor Me with their lips but remove their hearts and minds far from Me, and their fear and reverence for Me are a commandment of men that is learned by repetition [without any thought as to the meaning]" (Isaiah 29:13)

Your Father wants you to do more than just honor Him with your mouth. He wants your heart and your mind to be totally committed to Him. He wants you to understand what fear and reverence for Him is and to obey His specific instructions in regard to fearing Him and revering Him. Do not make the mistake of doing what some Christians and all unbelievers do. They are "...lovers of sensual pleasures and

vain amusements more than and rather than lovers of God."
(II Timothy 3:4)

We are not saying that you cannot enjoy wholesome pleasure. We are saying that God does not want you to love any
worldly source of pleasure more than you love Him. God
will bless you if you turn away from this kind of lifestyle.
"…not going your own way or seeking or finding your own
pleasure or speaking with your own [idle] words, then will
you delight yourself in the Lord, and I will make you to ride
on the high places of the earth…" (Isaiah 58:13-14)

God wants you to live the way that He instructs you to
live instead of going your own way. He does not want you to
speak idle words about being a Christian. Your Father wants
your life to be totally and completely committed to Him. Your
Father will bless you abundantly if you make this commitment.

God instructs you to love Him more than you love the
members of your family. Jesus Christ said, "If anyone comes
to Me and does not hate his [own] father and mother [in the
sense of indifference to or relative disregard for them in com-
parison with his attitude toward God] and [likewise] his wife
and children and brothers and sisters—[yes] and even his
own life also—he cannot be My disciple." (Luke 14:26)

Jesus talks about having a relative disregard for your parents compared to your commitment to God. He says that you
should have the same relative disregard for your wife and
children and brothers and sisters and even for yourself if you
sincerely desire to revere God and serve Him.

The truth is that you will be a *better* father or mother or
husband or wife if you consistently place your reverent awe
for God ahead of your love for members of your family. Your
family will *not* suffer if you put God first. Just the opposite

will be true. Keeping God first ahead of everyone and everything else is a positive, not a negative.

If your life is totally committed to doing what God has instructed you to do to live in reverent awe of Him, your personal life and your relationship with your family will be much better than if you only have a surface relationship with God. Jesus said, "He who loves [and takes more pleasure in] father or mother more than [in] Me is not worthy of Me; and he who loves [and takes more pleasure in] son or daughter more than [in] Me is not worthy of Me; and he who does not take up his cross and follow Me [cleave steadfastly to Me, conforming wholly to My example in living and, if need be, in dying also] is not worthy of Me. Whoever finds his [lower] life will lose it [the higher life], and whoever loses his [lower] life on My account will find it [the higher life]." (Matthew 10:37-39)

Jesus instructs you not to take more pleasure in the members of your family than you do in Him. He instructs you to conform to His example of total commitment to God. Jesus explains that you will find the higher life that God has for you if you obey these instructions.

We are making some strong statements here. The lifestyle that we are recommending is very different from the way that many Christians live. We are not merely giving our opinion. Each of these recommendations is solidly anchored on the Word of God.

Make the total commitment to fear and revere God throughout the remainder of your life. Turn away from focusing on accumulating wealth, the pursuit of pleasure and anything else that you may have allowed to come ahead of God. "…pursue that consecration and holiness without which no one will [ever] see the Lord." (Hebrews 12:14)

The word "consecration" in this verse means to devote your life entirely to reverent awe of God. God is sacred. He is holy. If you truly want to live in reverent awe of God, you will devote your life to doing what your Father has instructed you to do. This book is filled with these specific instructions from God.

The life of holiness that is called for in this verse is a totally dedicated life that does not allow anyone or anything to come ahead of God in any way. The Bible speaks of "...those who deal with this world [overusing the enjoyments of this life] as though they were not absorbed by it and as if they had no dealings with it..." (I Corinthians 7:31)

Your Father instructs you to turn away from the world. Turn away from preoccupation with worldly pleasures. Turn away from being absorbed with anything that you are pursuing ahead of total reverence and awe for God.

Jesus Christ paid a tremendous price for your sins. He also paid this price to deliver you from living the way that many people in the world live. The Bible speaks of "...our Lord Jesus Christ (the Messiah), Who gave (yielded) Himself up [to atone] for our sins [and to save and sanctify us], in order to rescue and deliver us from this present wicked age and world order, in accordance with the will and purpose and plan of our God and Father" (Galatians 1:3-4)

Jesus Christ died on the cross at Calvary to rescue you from the wickedness that is in the world. "...Turn away from the irreverent babble and godless chatter, with the vain and empty and worldly phrases, and the subtleties and the contradictions in what is falsely called knowledge and spiritual illumination. [For] by making such profession some have erred (missed the mark) as regards the faith." (I Timothy 6:20-21)

The world today consists primarily of surface relationships that are characterized by "irreverent babble and godless chatter." Many people live "vain and empty lives" because they are not committed to God. Do not make the mistake of living a worldly life even though you may be a professed Christian and living a moral life. "...Do you not know that being the world's friend is being God's enemy? So whoever chooses to be a friend of the world takes his stand as an enemy of God." (James 4:4)

Many Christians live good, moral lives, but they still are living worldly lives. Their lives revolve primarily around people, places and events in the world instead of revolving around reverent awe for God. The Bible says that these people are enemies of God. "Do not love or cherish the world or the things that are in the world. If anyone loves the world, love for the Father is not in him." (I John 2:15)

Do not love anyone or anything in the world more than you love God (see Matthew 22:37-38). You cannot live in reverent awe of God without being totally committed to Him. Jesus said, "...you are not of the world [no longer one with it], but I have chosen (selected) you out of the world" (John 15:19)

If Jesus Christ is your Savior, He has chosen you out of the world. He does not want you to be worldly. Turn away from all worldliness in your life, no matter how clean and moral this lifestyle may seem. Make the commitment to live in reverent awe of God with a lifestyle that puts God first at all times ahead of everone and everything else.

This world is not your home. You may be a citizen of a particular country, but if Jesus Christ is your Savior, you actually are a citizen of heaven. "...we are citizens of the state (commonwealth, homeland) which is in heaven..." (Philippians 3:20)

Identify with your citizenship in heaven, not with your citizenship wherever you live on earth. Make the decision to live in total commitment to God as you revere Him in every area of your life. The Bible says that all Christians are "...aliens and strangers and exiles [in this world]..." (I Peter 2:11)

The more that you comprehend how great, magnificent and awesome God is, the more you will turn away from everything in the world to turn more and more toward God. Your life will steadily become what God wants it to be.

Chapter 13

Trust God Completely

In Chapter 10 we briefly studied Scripture pertaining to the relationship between pride, humility and living in reverent awe of God. In this chapter we will study additional Scripture pertaining to pride and humility. God does not want you to be proud. "...do not become proud and conceited, but rather stand in awe and be reverently afraid." (Romans 11:20)

Please note that this verse of Scripture contrasts pride and reverent awe of God. Proud people do not have reverent awe for God. God loves *everyone* on earth unconditionally (see Psalm 33:5 and Romans 8:1). Nevertheless, God takes a strong stand against people who are proud. "...God sets Himself against the proud (the insolent, the overbearing, the disdainful, the presumptuous, the boastful)—[and He opposes, frustrates, and defeats them], but gives grace (favor, blessing) to the humble." (I Peter 5:5)

The amplification in this verse says that God "opposes, frustrates and defeats" people who are proud, boastful and overbearing. Can you imagine placing yourself in a position where Almighty God will oppose, frustrate and defeat you? This is exactly what proud people do.

This verse goes on to say that God gives grace, favor and blessing to His children who are humble. God promises to bless His children abundantly who live their lives based on reverent awe for Him. These blessings are reserved for humble children of God because only humble Christians will live in continual reverent awe of God. Jesus Christ said, "Whoever exalts himself [with haughtiness and empty pride] shall be humbled (brought low), and whoever humbles himself [whoever has a modest opinion of himself and behaves accordingly] shall be raised to honor." (Matthew 23:12)

The word "whoever" that is used twice in this verse refers to every person who is proud and every person who is humble. Every person who is consistently proud ultimately will be brought down. Every person who is consistently humble ultimately will be raised up by God.

There is no question that God does *not* want you to be proud. Your Father wants to help you, guide you and teach you. He will give you these blessings to the degree that you humble yourself before Him. "He leads the humble in what is right, and the humble He teaches His way." (Psalm 25:9)

Get out of the driver's seat. Give up control of your life. Keep God in first place at all times. God said, "You shall have no other gods before or besides Me." (Exodus 20:3)

Some Christians have other gods ahead of God. The god for some Christians is their vocation. Some Christians' god is accumulating wealth. Some people's god is an athletic team, a hobby or something else that they allow to come ahead of reverent awe for God.

You will only revere God to the degree that He truly is in first place in every area of your life. The following verse of Scripture refers to keeping Jesus Christ in first place in your life. "He also is the Head of [His] body, the church; seeing He is the Beginning, the Firstborn from among the dead, so that He alone in everything and in every respect might occupy the chief place [stand first and be preeminent]." (Colossians 1:18)

When Jesus rose from death, He overcame death for you. He died for your sins. He earned the right to be in first place in every area of your life. "None of us lives to himself [but to the Lord], and none of us dies to himself [but to the Lord, for] if we live, we live to the Lord, and if we die, we die to the Lord. So then, whether we live or we die, we belong to the Lord. For Christ died and lived again for this very purpose, that He might be Lord both of the dead and of the living." (Romans 14:7-9)

Please note that the word "none" is used two times in this passage of Scripture. No person should be in first place in his or her life. Your life belongs to Jesus Christ for the tremendous price that He paid for you.

Jesus Christ, Who is one with God and equal to God (see Philippians 2:5-8), left His exalted position in heaven to come to earth as a human being to be crucified at Calvary to offer up His life for you. He paid the full price for the sins of every person in the world. There is no question that Jesus has earned the right to be in first place in every aspect of your life.

Do not allow anyone or anything in the world to come ahead of Christ. Going to church once or twice a week and praying for a few minutes each day is not enough. Every aspect of your life should revolve around the intimacy of your relationship with God. Jesus said, "...seek (aim at and strive after) first of all His kingdom and His righteousness (His way of doing and being right), and then all these things taken together will be given you besides." (Matthew 6:33)

When Jesus spoke these words in the Sermon on the Mount, He was referring to the basic needs of life. Jesus was referring to such things as food and clothing when He said that "all these things" will be given to you. Jesus instructs you to put God first and to keep him first in every area of your life. Be like the psalmist who said, "...I have no delight or desire on earth besides You." (Psalm 73:25)

Make the quality decision to live in reverent awe of God so that He will be ahead of anyone or anything else in your life. Focus totally, completely and absolutely on God. "...set your mind and heart to seek (inquire of and require as your vital necessity) the Lord your God...." (I Chronicles 22:19)

The amplification of this verse says that keeping God in first place in your life is a "vital necessity." Focusing on God and keeping Him first is essential to living in reverent awe of God. "...[earnestly] remember the Lord and imprint Him [on your minds]..." (Nehemiah 4:14)

When you do something earnestly, you are very focused on whatever you are doing. Imprint God on your mind. Focus on your deep, strong and intense desire to live in reverent awe of God. "...set your minds and keep them set on what is above (the higher things), not on the things that are on the earth." (Colossians 3:2)

This verse instructs you to set your mind and to keep it set on God. Keep God in first place ahead of everyone and everything on earth.

You saw in Chapter 11 that God will bless you abundantly if you truly fear and revere Him and keep Him in first place in your life. The scriptural instructions that we are explaining in this chapter may seem severe. They are just the opposite. If you commit to keeping God in first place in your life and if you live your life in reverent awe of Him, you will place yourself in a spiritual position to be used mightily by God. Follow the example of the psalmist David who said, "I have set the Lord continually before me; because He is at my right hand, I shall not be moved." (Psalm 16:8)

David kept the Lord in first place at all times. He was continually conscious that God lived in his heart and that God was with him throughout every minute of every hour of every day of his life. At a later time David said, "My eyes are ever toward the Lord..." (Psalm 25:15)

Please note the word "ever" in this verse. David consistently kept God in first place in his life. If you truly fear and revere God, you will focus on Him continually. You will make the quality decision not to allow anyone or anything to distract you from keeping God in first place in your life at all times.

If God truly is in first place in your life, you will not complain. God was not pleased when He heard the Israelites complaining when they were in the wilderness. "...the people grumbled and deplored their hardships, which was evil in the ears of the Lord..." (Numbers 11:1)

Why would you ever grumble and complain about anything if God truly is in first place in your life and you are absolutely certain that your loving Father will take care of you? When the Israelites complained, Moses said, "...the Lord has heard your grumblings which you murmur against Him..." (Exodus 16:8)

Whenever you grumble, gripe and complain, you actually are complaining *against God*. Complaining shows that God is not in first place in your life. If God is in first place and if you trust Him completely, you will not complain. "Do all things without grumbling and faultfinding and complaining [against God] and questioning and doubting [among yourselves]" (Philippians 2:14)

Please note the words "all things" in this verse. God does not want you to ever grumble, gripe, find fault or complain. The amplification in this verse once again explains that every person who complains actually is complaining against God. "At all times and for everything giving thanks in the name of our Lord Jesus Christ to God the Father." (Ephesians 5:20)

Instead of complaining, you are instructed to thank God at all times. You are instructed to thank God for everything in the name of Jesus Christ. "Thank [God] in everything [no matter what the circumstances may be, be thankful and give thanks], for this is the will of God for you [who are] in Christ Jesus [the Revealer and Mediator of that will].' (I Thessalonians 5:18)

This verse and the amplification instruct you to thank God in everything, "no matter what the circumstances may be." Thank God at all times regardless of what is happening in your life. God wants you to be absolutely certain that He is in complete control. He wants you to honor Him, to revere Him, to keep Him first and to trust Him completely.

If these words describe your attitude toward God, you will thank God at all times, no matter what circumstances you face. Why wouldn't you thank God if you are absolutely certain that He will be with you in whatever problems you face? "...thanks be to God, Who in Christ always leads us in triumph [as trophies of Christ's victory]..." (II Corinthians 2:14)

God always does what He says He will do (see Joshua 23:14, I Corinthians 1:9 and II Corinthians 1:20). If God promises to *always* give you victory over whatever problems you face, why wouldn't you thank Him?

God promises to give you the victory, but He does not tell you *when* this will happen. Do not give up. Keep on revering God. Keep on thanking Him. Know that your loving Father will give you manifestation of the glorious victory that Jesus Christ won for you in His way and in His good timing.

Trust God's timing just as you trust Him in every other area. Revere Him. Fear Him. Honor Him. Keep Him in first place in your life even if nothing seems to be happening. Know that God will bring you safely through every problem you face. Thank God continually for giving you manifestation of the victory that Jesus Christ won for you.

Chapter 14

Reverent Awe for God and Your Lifestyle

In the last chapter we studied Scripture about keeping God first in your life, focusing on God and thanking God continually. In this chapter we will study additional scriptural instructions about the lifestyle that God wants you to live if you truly have reverent awe for Him. We will begin this chapter with a topic that is similar to giving thanks to God – praising God. If you have great reverence for God, you will praise Him continually. "You who fear (revere and worship) the Lord, praise Him!..." (Psalm 22:23)

If you knew that God created you for a specific purpose, wouldn't you be highly motivated to carry out this purpose? God created you to praise Him. He said, "The people I formed for Myself, that they may set forth My praise [and they shall do it]." (Isaiah 43:21)

The amplification of this verse instructs you to do what God created you to do. You bless your Father when you do what He created you to do. If you truly fear God, you will be highly motivated to bless Him by praising Him often. "...you who reverently and worshipfully fear the Lord, bless the Lord [affectionately and gratefully praise Him]!" (Psalm 135:20)

God blesses each of His children in many ways. You have an opportunity to bless Him in return. Is your heart filled with gratitude to God? If so, show your affection and gratitude to God by praising Him. God instructs every person on earth to praise Him. "Let everything that has breath and every breath of life praise the Lord! Praise the Lord!..." (Psalm 150:6)

The words "everything that has breath" include you. The Bible instructs you to praise God continually. "From the rising of the sun to the going down of it and from east to west, the name of the Lord is to be praised!" (Psalm 113:3)

God instructs you to praise Him continually wherever you are. If you have reverent awe for God, praising Him will be a way of life to you. "...let us constantly and at all times offer up to God a sacrifice of praise, which is the fruit of lips that thankfully acknowledge and confess and glorify His name." (Hebrews 13:15)

Please note the words "a sacrifice of praise" in this verse. When you face adversity, make the sacrifice of praising God even though you may be facing severe problems.

You are instructed to glorify the name of God by praising Him. You saw in the last chapter that God instructs you to thank Him at all times regardless of the circumstances you face (see Ephesians 5:20 and I Thessalonians 5:18). God also instructs you to praise Him continually regardless of the circumstances you face.

Do not limit your praise to God to the times when everything is going well. If you have great reverence and awe for God, you will praise Him continually. You will be like the psalmist David who said, "I will bless the Lord at all times; His praise shall continually be in my mouth." (Psalm 34:1)

You bless God when you praise Him continually. You also bless your Father when you pray often to Him. "...the prayer of the upright is His delight!" (Proverbs 15:8)

People who are righteous before God are upright. If Jesus Christ is your Savior, you are righteous before God because all of your sins have been cleansed by the shed blood of Jesus Christ. Your Father is *delighted* when you come to Him in prayer.

You have seen that you bless God by praising Him continually. You have seen that God is delighted when you pray to Him. Show your reverent awe for God by praying constantly. "Be unceasing in prayer [praying perseveringly]" (I Thessalonians 5:17)

God instructs you to persevere in your prayers to Him. If you do not receive God's answer as soon as you would like, keep on praying. Jesus said, "...I say to you, Ask and keep on asking and it shall be given you; seek and keep on seeking and you shall find; knock and keep on knocking and the door shall be opened to you. For everyone who asks and keeps on asking receives; and he who seeks and keeps on seeking finds; and to him who knocks and keeps on knocking, the door shall be opened." (Luke 11:9-10)

The words "keep on" and "keeps on" are used six times in this passage of Scripture. There is no question that God wants you to persevere when you pray in faith. God always does what His Word says He will do (see I Corinthians 1:9). When you pray, consider the prayer answered if you know that you have prayed according to God's will and in Jesus' name. Continue to thank God for His answer. "...The earnest (heartfelt, continued) prayer of a righteous man makes tremendous power available [dynamic in its working]." (James 5:16)

This verse says that, if you continually pray from your heart, you will release tremendous power in the spiritual realm. Jesus said, "If you live in Me [abide vitally united to Me] and My words remain in you and continue to live in your hearts, ask whatever you will, and it shall be done for you." (John 15:7)

The words "abide vitally united to Me" in the amplification of this verse show the importance of staying close to Jesus and centering your life around your absolute certainty of His indwelling presence (see II Corinthians 13:5, Galatians 2:20, Ephesians 3:1, I John 2:15-16 and I John 3:24). Pray to God based on specific promises in the Bible. Know that God *will* answer your prayer in His perfect timing.

You can be certain that God has a specific plan for every day of your life. Pray asking God to reveal what He has for you to do each day. "…we are God's [own] handiwork (His workmanship), recreated in Christ Jesus, [born anew] that we may do those good works which God predestined (planned beforehand) for us [taking paths which He prepared ahead of time], that we should walk in them [living the good life which He prearranged and made ready for us to live]." (Ephesians 2:10)

Is Jesus Christ your Savior? If He is, you have been born again in the Spirit of God to complete the specific assignment that God has for your life. This verse speaks of doing what God has called you to do. If you truly revere God, you will be highly motivated to do what He has called you to do with your life. Jesus said, "…Your will be done [held holy and revered] on earth as it is in heaven." (Luke 11:2)

These words are part of the Lord's Prayer. Everyone in heaven reveres God. This verse and the amplification say that God's will is meant to be "revered on earth as it is in heaven."

If you truly revere God, you will place absolute priority on seeking, finding and successfully completing His plan for your life. Every person in heaven does what God wants them to do. Have a deep and sincere desire that you will have consistent reverence for God by seeking His will for your life. "...do not be vague and thoughtless and foolish, but understanding and firmly grasping what the will of the Lord is." (Ephesians 5:17)

Make the commitment to consistently seek God's plan for your life. Do not waste your life doing things that are "vague and thoughtless and foolish." Show your reverence for your Father by constantly praying to Him asking Him to reveal every aspect of His assignment for your life.

Once again, if you are interested in more information on finding God's will for your life, we recommend our book, *God's Plan for Your Life.* This book is solidly anchored on 241 verses of Scripture with a simple and easy-to-understand explanation of each passage of Scripture.

If you have deep and reverent awe for God, you will devote your life to serving Him. You will stay close to Him at all times, trusting Him completely. "You shall [reverently] fear the Lord your God; you shall serve Him and cling to Him, and by His name and presence you shall swear." (Deuteronomy 10:20)

You serve God by doing what He has called you to do. You show your reverence and awe for God by consistently devoting your life to seeking, finding and carrying out His plan for your life. "...turn not aside from following the Lord, but serve Him with all your heart. And turn not aside after vain and worthless things which cannot profit or deliver you, for they are empty and futile." (I Samuel 12:20-21)

You are instructed to serve God wholeheartedly. You are warned not to waste your time on vain, worthless and empty things in the world. "...fear the Lord and serve Him faithfully with all your heart; for consider how great are the things He has done for you." (I Samuel 12:24)

If you truly have reverent fear for God, you will serve Him faithfully with all your heart. God has done great things for you. Devote your life to serving Him in every way that you can. "Serve the Lord with reverent awe and worshipful fear..." (Psalm 2:11)

This verse explains the relationship between reverent awe for God and serving God. God is very pleased with His children who reverently fear Him and devote their lives to serving Him instead of pursuing personal desires.

If you devote your life to serving God, your life will be full, meaningful and complete. God created us in such a way that we will only experience deep meaning and fulfillment in our lives by doing what He created us to do. Follow the example of the apostle Paul who said, "...I die daily [I face death every day and die to self]." (I Corinthians 15:31)

Turn away from personal desires. Die to all selfish desires. Commit yourself to showing your reverent awe for God by devoting your life to serving Him and carrying out His assignment for your life.

Willingly give up your God-given right to control your own life. Continually yield control of your life to the Holy Spirit Who lives in the heart of every person who has received Jesus Christ as his or her Savior (see Galatians 4:6). "...you are living the life of the Spirit, if the [Holy] Spirit of God [really] dwells within you [directs and controls you]...." (Romans 8:9)

Show your reverent awe for God by willingly yielding control of your life to the Holy Spirit to guide you throughout every day of your life. "...walk and live [habitually] in the [Holy] Spirit [responsive to and controlled and guided by the Spirit]..." (Galatians 5:16)

Please not the word "habitually" in the amplification of this verse. Show your reverent awe for God by consistently yielding control of your life to the Holy Spirit. "...[the determination of] the way of a man is not in himself; it is not in man [even in a strong man or in a man at his best] to direct his [own] steps." (Jeremiah 10:23)

Do not depend on yourself and whatever talent and ability God has given to you. Pray for the Holy Spirit to guide you throughout every moment of each day. Yield your will to the Holy Spirit throughout the day. As you do this over a period of time, you will grow in your degree of surrender as you experience more and more of the magnificent grace and favor of God.

This chapter has been devoted to showing your reverent awe for God by praising Him, by constant prayer, by seeking His will for your life, by serving Him continually and by consistently yielding control of your life to the Holy Spirit. If you obey the scriptural instructions in this chapter, you will constantly show your reverence and awe for God. You will be living the way that God created you to live.

Conclusion

This book is filled with Scripture references that explain reverent awe for God. In Chapter 1 we explained the omnipotence, omniscience and omnipresence of God. How can anyone not have reverent awe for God if they even begin to comprehend how great, awesome and magnificent He is?

In Chapter 2 we studied Scripture that explains that the same God Who created everyone and everything in the entire universe lives in your heart if Jesus Christ is your Savior. You truly will live in reverent awe of God if you are certain that the Creator of the universe lives in your heart and that He is with you throughout every day of your life.

God is great and mighty. He is more than worthy of your reverent awe. God created you to fear Him and revere Him. Your Father wants you to consistently study and meditate on His Book of Instructions, the Bible, so that you will learn how to live a life of reverent awe for Him.

We devoted two chapters to explaining the relationship between receiving God's supernatural wisdom and having reverent awe for God. Your Father will bless you abundantly if you show your reverent awe for Him by devoting your life to doing what He has called you to do.

We devoted a chapter to explaining the many blessings that God will pour out upon you if you live a life of reverent awe for Him. The final three chapters are filled with Scripture that explains exactly how God instructs you to live if you truly are in reverent awe of Him.

We pray that this book has helped you to live a life of reverent awe for God. Please pray about sharing a copy of this book with other Christians who will be interested in learning what God has said about living in reverent awe of Him.

Take advantage of the quantity discounts that we offer. From our beginning God has instructed us to give our readers similar discounts to the ones that bookstores receive when they purchase books in quantity. The order form at the back of this book explains these discounts.

If this book has helped you, would you share your testimony with us so that we can share with others what you have learned about reverent awe of God? We normally need three to four paragraphs in a testimony so that we can consolidate this information into one solid paragraph for our newsletter and our website. Your comments will encourage many people, including pastors and leaders in Third World countries and inmates in prisons and jails who receive our books free of charge.

Please send any comments that you have to us at lamplightmin@yahoo.com. You can call 1-800-540-1597 and leave a message for Judy. You also can mail your comments to Lamplight Ministries, Inc., PO Box 1307, Dunedin, FL 34697.

The following pages contain selected comments from the thousands of comments we have received from people in more than 60 countries who have been helped by our books and Scripture cards.

You can download the first chapter of each book. You can leave prayer requests that Judy will see immediately. She will begin praying for you and she will send your request to our prayer warriors.

We invite you to visit our website: www.lamplight.net. You will find many additional comments from people who have been helped by our books and Scripture cards. You also will find a section on biblical health as well as recipes that Judy adds each month to bless you. We are in good health at ages 82 and 74. I know that I would not be alive today if it were not for Judy's knowledge and wisdom regarding health and her amazing recipes.

You can keep in touch with us on Facebook (facebook.com/jackandjudylamplight) and Twitter (twitter.com/lamplightmin). You can follow our blog at lamplightmin.wordpress.com You can receive frequent updates on our latest books.

We have been blessed to share with you the results of hundreds of hours of effort that we have invested to explain what the Word of God says about reverent awe of God. We are excited to hear about your journey with Jesus Christ through this book. We would be so pleased to hear from you.

Blessed to be a blessing. (Genesis 12:1-3)

Jack and Judy

Appendix

Trusting in Jesus Christ as Your Savior

This book is filled with instructions and promises from God. However, if you have not received Jesus Christ as your Savior, you *cannot understand* the scriptural truths that are contained in this book. "...the mind of the flesh [with its carnal thoughts and purposes] is hostile to God, for it does not submit itself to God's Law; indeed it cannot." (Romans 8:7)

Please notice the word "cannot" in this verse of Scripture. If Jesus is not your Savior, you cannot understand and obey God's instructions.

Many people who have not received Jesus Christ as their Savior are not open to the specific instructions that God has given to us in the Bible. "...the natural, nonspiritual man does not accept or welcome or admit into his heart the gifts and teachings and revelations of the Spirit of God, for they are folly (meaningless nonsense) to him; and he is incapable of knowing them [of progressively recognizing, understanding, and becoming better acquainted with them] because they are spiritually discerned and estimated and appreciated." (I Corinthians 2:14)

The words "does not accept or welcome or admit into his heart the gifts and teachings and revelations of the Spirit of God" in this verse of Scripture are very important. Some people are strongly opposed to the Bible and what it teaches. They look at Scripture references from the Bible as "meaningless nonsense." These people are incapable of learning great scriptural truths from God until and unless they receive Jesus Christ as their Savior.

At the close of this Appendix we will explain exactly what God instructs you to do to receive Jesus Christ as your Savior. If and when you make this decision, the glorious supernatural truths of the Bible will open up to you. Jesus said, "...To you it has been given to know the secrets and mysteries of the kingdom of heaven, but to them it has not been given." (Matthew 13:11)

Jesus was speaking to *you* when He said that you can "know the secrets and mysteries of the kingdom of heaven." Do not miss out on the glorious privilege that is available to every believer to know and understand the ways of God.

A spiritual veil blocks all unbelievers from understanding the things of God. "...even if our Gospel (the glad tidings) also be hidden (obscured and covered up with a veil that hinders the knowledge of God), it is hidden [only] to those who are perishing and obscured [only] to those who are spiritually dying and veiled [only] to those who are lost." (II Corinthians 4:3)

When and if you receive Jesus Christ as your Savior, this spiritual veil is pulled aside. "...whenever a person turns [in repentance] to the Lord, the veil is stripped off and taken away." (II Corinthians 3:16)

If you obey the scriptural instructions at the end of this Appendix, Jesus Christ will become your Savior. Everything in your life will become fresh and new. "...if any person is [ingrafted] in Christ (the Messiah) he is a new creation (a new creature altogether); the old [previous moral and spiritual condition] has passed away. Behold, the fresh and new has come!" (II Corinthians 5:17)

Instead of being opposed to the teachings of the holy Bible, you will be completely open to these teachings. You will have a hunger and thirst to continually learn more supernatural truths from the Word of God. "...I endorse and delight in the Law of God in my inmost self [with my new nature]." (Romans 7:22)

Every person who has not received Jesus Christ as his or her Savior is a sinner who is doomed to live throughout eternity in the horror of hell. God has made it possible for *you* to escape this terrible eternal penalty. "...God so greatly loved and dearly prized the world that He [even] gave up His only begotten (unique) Son, so that whoever believes in (trusts in, clings to, relies on) Him shall not perish (come to destruction, be lost) but have eternal (everlasting) life." (John 3:16)

God knew that everyone who lived on earth after Adam and Eve would be a sinner because of the sins of Adam and Eve (see Romans 3:10-12). He sent His only Son to take upon Himself the sins of the world as He died a horrible death by crucifixion. If you believe that Jesus Christ paid the full price for *your* sins and if you trust Him completely for your eternal salvation, you will live with Him eternally in the glory of heaven.

There is only *one* way for you to live eternally in heaven after you die – that is to receive eternal salvation through Jesus Christ. "Jesus said to him, I am the Way and the Truth and the Life; no one comes to the Father except by (through) Me." (John 14:6)

If you trust in anyone or anything except Jesus Christ for your eternal salvation, you will not live eternally in heaven. If you are reading these truths about living eternally in heaven because of the price that Jesus Christ has paid for you, you can be certain that the same God Who created you actually is drawing you to come to Jesus Christ for eternal salvation. Jesus said, "No one is able to come to Me unless the Father Who sent Me attracts and draws him and gives him the desire to come to Me…" (John 6:44)

Are you interested in these spiritual truths about where you will live throughout eternity? If you are, you can be certain that the same awesome God Who created you is drawing *you* to Jesus Christ at this very moment.

Heaven is a glorious place. Everyone in heaven is completely healthy and very happy. "God will wipe away every tear from their eyes; and death shall be no more, neither shall there be anguish (sorrow and mourning) nor grief nor pain any more, for the old conditions and the former order of things have passed away." (Revelation 21:4)

All of the problems of earth will disappear when you arrive in heaven. No one in heaven dies. No one in heaven is sad. No one in heaven cries. No one in heaven suffers from pain.

You *will* live throughout eternity in one place or another after you die. If you do not receive Jesus Christ as your Savior, you will live eternally in hell. People in hell will experience continual torment throughout eternity. "…the smoke of their torment ascends forever and ever; and they have no respite (no pause, no intermission, no rest, no peace) day or night…" (Revelation 14:11)

Everyone in heaven is filled with joy. Everyone in hell is miserable. Jesus described what hell would be like when He said, "…there will be weeping and wailing and grinding of teeth. (Matthew 13:42)

Throughout eternity the inhabitants of hell will weep and wail. They will grind their teeth in anguish. Can you imagine living this way for the endless trillions of years of eternity? This is exactly what will happen if you *reject* the supreme sacrifice that Jesus Christ made to pay the full price for your sins.

How do you receive eternal salvation through Jesus Christ? "…if you acknowledge and confess with your lips that Jesus is Lord and in your heart believe (adhere to, trust in, and rely on the truth) that God raised Him from the dead, you will be saved. For with the heart a person believes (adheres to, trusts in, and relies on Christ) and so is justified (declared righteous, acceptable to God), and with the mouth he confesses (declares openly and speaks out freely his faith) and confirms [his] salvation." (Romans 10:9-10)

Repent of your sins. You must *believe in your heart* (not just think in your mind) that Jesus Christ paid the full price for all of your sins when He was crucified. You must believe that God actually raised Jesus from the dead. You must open your mouth and *speak* this truth that you believe in your heart. If you believe in your heart that Jesus Christ died and rose again from the dead and that the price for your sins has been paid for and you tell others that you believe this great spiritual truth, you *have* been saved. You *will* live eternally in heaven.

If Jesus Christ was not your Savior when you began to read this book, we pray that He is your Savior now. Your life will change immensely. You will never be the same again. Every aspect of your life will be gloriously new.

If you have become a child of God by receiving eternal salvation through Jesus Christ, please let us know by contacting us at lamplightmin@yahoo.com, 1-800-540-1497 or PO Box 1307, Dunedin, FL 34697. We would like to pray for you and welcome you as our new Christian brother or sister. We love you and bless you in the name of our Lord Jesus Christ.

We would be so pleased to hear from you. If you are already a believer, we would be pleased to hear from you as well. We invite you to visit our website at www.lamplight.net. Please let us know if this book or one or more of our other publications has made a difference in our life. Please give us your comments so that we can share these comments in our newsletters and on our website to encourage other people.

Study Guide

What Did You Learn From This Book?

The questions in this Study Guide are carefully arranged to show you how much you have learned about reverent awe for God. This Study Guide is not intended to be an academic test. The sole purpose of the following questions is to help you increase your practical knowledge pertaining to reverent awe for God.

A Few Words About Lamplight Ministries

Lamplight Ministries, Inc. originally began in 1983 as Lamplight Publications. After ten years as a publishing firm with a goal of selling Christian books, Lamplight Ministries was established in 1993. Jack and Judy Hartman founded Lamplight Ministries with a mission of continuing to sell their publications and also to give large numbers of these publications free of charge to needy people all over the world.

Lamplight Ministries was created to allow people who have been blessed by our publications to share in financing the translation, printing and distribution of our books into other languages and also to distribute our publications free of charge to inmates in jails and prisons. Over the years many partners of Lamplight Ministries have shared Jack and Judy's vision. Thousands of people in jails and prisons and in Third World countries have received our publications free of charge.

Our books and Scripture Meditation Cards have been translated into eleven foreign languages – Armenian, Danish, Greek, Hebrew, German, Korean, Norwegian, Portuguese, Russian, Spanish and the Tamil dialect in India. The translations in these languages are not available from Lamplight Ministries in the United States. These translations can only be obtained in the countries where we have given permission for them to be published.

The pastors of many churches in Third World countries have written to say that they consistently preach sermons in their churches based on the scriptural contents of our publications. We believe that people in several churches in many different countries consistently hear sermons that are based on the scriptural contents of our publications. Praise the Lord!

Jack Hartman was the sole author of twelve Christian books. After co-authoring one book with Judy, Jack and Judy co-authored ten sets of Scripture Meditation Cards. Judy has been the co-author of every subsequent book. Jack and Judy currently are working on other books that they believe the Lord is leading them to write as co-authors.

We invite you to request our newsletters to stay in touch with us, to learn of our latest publications and to read comments from people all over the world. Please write, fax, call or email us. You are very special to us. We love you and thank God for you. Our heart is to take the gospel to the world and for our books to be available in every known language. Hallelujah!

Lamplight Ministries, Inc.,

PO Box 1307 - Dunedin, Florida, 34697. USA

Phone: 1-800-540-1597 • Fax: 1-727-784-2980

website: lamplight.net • email: lamplightmin@yahoo.com

Enthusiastic Comments from Readers of Our Publications

The following are just a few of the many comments we have received from people in more than 60 countries pertaining to our publications. For additional comments, see our website: lamplight.net.

Trust God for Your Finances

There are more than 150,000 copies of *Trust God for Your Finances* in print. This book has been translated into seven foreign languages.

- "I have translated *Trust God for Your Finances* into Thai. I intended to make about 50 or 60 photocopies of this translation to distribute among friends. My pastor asked for 700 copies to distribute at the special yearly conference for pastors. My immediate thought was that I could not do this, but he urged me to pray and try my best. Surprisingly, it worked out. Thank God. More than 1,000 people attended the conference. Seven hundred copies were distributed to only the pastors, elders and deacons who really wanted the book. After the conference, we had so many calls that another 2,000 copies were printed. Thank you, Mr. Hartman, for this book which is helping so many Thai Christians." (Thailand)

- "I bought your book, *Trust God for Your Finances,* at a church I was attending in Virginia in the 1980s. This book transformed my life. It was all Bible-based and solid in every way. I married a Bulgarian pastor who started the church here during Communism and the underground church. We have pastored together for 22 years. I gave your book to my husband and he consumed it. He kept it near his Bible all the time. God has raised him up to be influential in this nation. He has written a book titled *The Covenant of Provision* dealing with finances. Your book helped him so much to form his ideas about the rightful use of money. This book has influenced my husband more than almost any other book. It was so timely and needed coming out of a Communist society. Thank you so much for this book." (Bulgaria)
- "Today we had a ministry partner join us for lunch. He said that the book, *Trust God for Your Finances*, that we had translated into Hebrew was the most powerful book he had ever read on the subject. I shared with him the wonderful story of how you shared the book with us and how many Israelis have been enlightened in that area as a result of reading the book. You both are a blessing and a treasure in God's kingdom." (Israel)

God's Instructions for Growing Older
- "I am a 63-year-old businesswoman from Thailand. Like most women around the world, I do not like growing old. When I received a copy of your book, *God's Instructions For Growing Olde*r, I read straight from the first page to the last in two days. Your book gives me the assurance of how to grow older without fear, anxiety, and worry. I will live the rest of my life in peace and joy for I now know that if we keep God in first place at all times, the final years of our lives will be meaningful, productive, and fulfilling. Thank you, Mr. and Mrs. Hartman, for the

priceless gift of your book. May God bless you and your team always." (Thailand)

- "I have never read a book like *God's Instructions for Growing Older*. Finally a book has been written that teaches how to finish our course in life as a Christian. Your chapter on Scripture meditation is pure gold. This book is a road map to direct us in the way the Lord intends for us to grow older. Thank you so much for this special book." (Florida)

- "Thank you for your new book, *God's Instructions for Growing Older.* I love this book. I read a little bit every day so that I can be an encourager to my older friends and to myself. We so need God's knowledge during the final years of our lives. I have started my gift list to share this book with others." (Texas)

You Can Hear the Voice of God

- "Many years of my life I scoffed at Christians. I looked at them as holy rollers. When I was incarcerated, I experienced pain as I have never felt in my life. A darkness and loneliness like I have never experienced before came upon me. A friend here gave me your book, *You Can Hear the Voice of God*. If there ever was a time when I needed to hear from God, it is now. My wife was desperately ill at the very point of death when I started reading your book. I now know that God has been trying to talk to me all of my life, but I didn't know how to listen to His voice. NOW I CAN HEAR THE VOICE OF GOD. In a splendid and simple way you actually taught me how to hear the voice of God Almighty. How can I ever thank you? Thank you for writing this book. It will impact hundreds of thousands, I am sure." (Florida)

- "Thank you for sending me a copy of *You Can Hear the Voice of God*. This book is so good. On the first day of having this book in my hands, I read continually. I finished five chapters. My wife was invited to teach at a meeting of pastors' wives. The women were excited because of this teaching. I would like to translate this book into Benba, one of the largest spoken languages on the copper belt and some provinces of Zambia. Would you give me permission to translate this book? I know that the Holy Spirit has inspired me to do so." (Permission was granted.) (Zambia)

- "Thank you for the box of books that you sent to a pastor who is a friend of mine. He gave me a copy of your book *You Can Hear The Voice of God*. This book is a spiritual manual for the serious Christian. I thank God for Jack and Judy Hartman. This book is helping me to draw closer to my Maker. I now realize that God has been talking to me daily but I did not hear Him. This book is a real blessing to the body of Christ." (Ghana)

Effective Prayer
- "I thank God for your book titled *Effective Prayer*. This book came to me at the right time. Since reading this book, God has done great wonders in my life and ministry. Our whole church is being affected by what we have learned about the power of prayer. I have read many books on prayer, but this one is unique. I no longer pray amiss. My prayer life has become much more effective. Your book has helped me to persevere in prayer much longer than before. This is a great book. I love it. I treasure this book. I do not know how to thank you. I pray that God will bless you both with long life and that you will enjoy the fruit of your labour." (Zambia)
- "Your book *Effective Prayer* is a great blessing to me. After reading this book I have so much more understanding about prayer. It is very easy to learn from all that you are teaching and all of the Scriptures in it. I now understand much more about the significance of

prayer in my daily life, why I should pray and how to pray. You have enlightened my mind. I know that my loving Father wants me to pray all the time. I have learned to pray God's answer instead of focusing on the problem. This book is very vital to my daily life. I am so thankful to both of you for another great book for people who need answers. Thank you so much for the great understanding that I found in this book." (the Philippines)

- "I have been studying your book *Effective Prayer.* This book has inspired me to do a lot more praying. Praying to God is such a privilege. To know that God is just waiting for me to come and talk with Him is tremendous. The way you brought out the gift of being baptized in the Holy Spirit and praying in tongues will make it easier for people to receive this much-needed gift in their lives. Our pastor is using your book to teach on prayer. I have given copies of this book to many people in our church. I gave one to another pastor in our town. I love you both in the Lord Jesus Christ. I thank God for you and for allowing Him to continue to use you in the body of Christ." (Oklahoma)

What Does God Say?

- "Your book *What Does God Say?* is one of the greatest books I have ever read. You tell the truth and back it up with Scripture. I started crime very young. I have spent a large portion of my life behind bars. I have so much to be ashamed of and things that I am very sorry for. I have almost wasted my life. I say almost because this book caused me to realize that God loves even me no matter what I have done. In your book I read that there is no condemnation in Christ Jesus. Do you have any idea what it means to feel no condemnation when society says to lock me up because I am guilty? My sins and all the crimes I have committed have been washed away. I cannot explain how it feels to know that someone is really proud of me. That someone is Jesus. I am taking this book home with me. Even though I don't have much education, I can understand it very well. I now know that I am saved and I am forgiven. Thank you very much for writing this book." (Florida)

- "Several months ago, you sent me a copy of your book titled *What Does God Say?*. This book is amazing. First of all, I could understand it. My English is not great. I have been a Muslim all my life. I was taught as a child what I was supposed to believe. When I was searching for real truth, I met the Master and received Jesus Christ as my Savior. When I read your book, it filled so much of the void and loneliness that I was filled with. I will be sharing Jesus and *What Does God Say?* with my family and with other Muslims. Please pray for me as I may not be welcomed in my own home town for finding this wonderful Jesus." (Ghana)

- "Our ministry here in South Africa is flourishing. We thank God for the books from Jack and Judy Hartman. The book, *What Does God Say?,* is my daily manual. It addresses all issues of life. I read it every day and I love it. I am complete. This book has made our ministry more effective. I no longer have to struggle on what to preach or teach. I am now equipped with the correct material. This book is filled with the anointing and revelation of God. My fellow pastors here in South Africa are hungry for these books. We soon will be opening a branch in Pretoria and also in Botswana. I thank God for the Hartmans. I always pray for them." (South Africa)

Quiet Confidence in the Lord
- "As soon as I was diagnosed with prostate cancer, I began to meditate on the Scripture and your explanation of the Scripture in *Quiet Confidence in the Lord.* I carried this

book with me everywhere for several weeks. The specialist at the Lahey Clinic in Boston told me I was the calmest person with this diagnosis that he had ever seen. During the pre-op and the surgery, a number of people commented on how calm I was. I experienced a lot of discomfort during the difficult first week at home after the surgery. I focused constantly on the Scripture in this wonderful book. I was remarkably calm. Thank you for writing this book that has helped me so much." (Massachusetts)

- "After I graduated from Bible school, I went outside of my country for mission work with my wife. After we were there for nine months, my wife died suddenly. My sorrow was great. I read your book titled *Quiet Confidence in the Lord*. This book spoke to my heart. All twenty-three chapters were written for me. God changed me through this book and comforted me and took away my sorrow. Through the blood of Jesus I entered God's rest. I can give a great recommendation for this book to anyone who is filled with sorrow and grief. I pray that many people will read this book and develop quiet confidence in the Lord as I did. Thank you so much for sending this book to me. May God bless you and your ministry." (Ethiopia)
- "*Quiet Confidence in the Lord* is with me at work each day. I have read and underlined passages that lift my heart and help me to understand something I've known all along and that is that I am not alone and that God cares very much that I'm in the midst of great adversity. I asked God to send me a comforter, someone who would put their arms around me and say, 'I understand and I care.' The answer to that prayer is in you and Judy. Thanks to *Quiet Confidence of the Lord* I am, for the first time in my life, learning to focus on God and not my problems. Thank you both for your ministry. Your books are a

tremendous blessing to hurting people all over the world."
(Washington, DC)

Receive Healing from the Lord

- "Your great book, *Receive Healing from the Lord*, has amazed me. This book has been my daily bread. I have followed all of God's instructions in your book. My children and my wife were healed from severe illness. I was sick myself just before an important crusade. I meditated on the Scripture in your book for the entire night. I was totally healed. The following day God did wonders as He healed many people. Since then, people have been coming to receive their healing at our home and church almost every day. Many healings are taking place at our services. This book is wonderful. I am abundantly blessed by it." (Zambia)
- "My husband and I served in the mission field in Swaziland, Africa, for three and a half years. Upon our arrival, Lamplight Ministries sent us four mailbags full of Jack and Judy's books. Because Swaziland is so laden with HIV/AIDS, we were able to use the book, *Receive Healing from the Lord*, with the people in Swaziland to see many people come to a saving knowledge of the Lord Jesus Christ and His perfect will regarding healing. We saw mothers with very sick children who themselves also were afflicted with AIDS respond to the many Scriptures that are part of the book, actually believing that it was meant for them. Had it not been for the use of this book and the other books you sent, we would not have had such success in teaching a Bible study about the truth in God's Word to these people. We gave out your books and told the people that the book was theirs to keep. We saw such joy and surprise on the faces of these impoverished people. We appreciate the ongoing generosity of Lamplight Ministries for 'such a time as this' in these

days where there is so much need and want. We will forever be thankful that we can count on the Word of God through the books written by Jack and Judy as effective tools in the transformation of people's lives." (Swaziland)

- "Thank you very much for sending me your book, *Receive Healing from the Lord.* After reading the first chapter I realized that this book could be the solution for my wife's failing health. We decided to read the book together every day. My wife was healed and restored after carefully following the scriptural principles that you explained. We are humbled by how we had struggled and panicked trying to find an answer. God gave us the solution in your book. We are so grateful to you. We love you and we are praying for you." (Zambia)

What Will Heaven Be Like?

- "On the very first page of your book on heaven I was spellbound. The material read so quickly and coherently that it was like having a conversation with a Christian friend. I could really feel the excitement as we talked about the throne of God and its radiance. Those who are curious about heaven will be so delighted and joyful when they read this book. I think the questions at the end of the book are a great idea. This book is a ready-made classroom treasure. I was deeply moved by the gentle loving approach and the manner this material was presented to me, the reader. I can hardly wait to read your other books. You have gained a new fan and admirer of your special way of presenting the kingdom of heaven and God's love for us." (Mississippi)
- "I came to China from Cambodia where I was a captain in the army. I was a Buddhist. Four weeks before I came to China, I had a dream where Jesus appeared to me. When I woke up the following morning, I looked for

Christians to explain more about Jesus Christ to me. After I came to China, I met a Christian man who gave me the book *What Will Heaven Be Like?*. This book answered many questions for me. My English is not very good, but this book is written in very simple English. I have found new life through this book. Please pray for me so that I can share Jesus with my parents and my Buddhist friends when I go back to Cambodia." (China)

- "I am the Youth Director of our church and I'm leading a group of high school students in a Bible study of your book on heaven. We all respect your opinions and have found your book to be an excellent springboard for discussion. It is thought-provoking and informative. This book has much substance and is well organized." (California)

Never, Never Give Up

- "I am a 68-year-old businessman. At my age I should be enjoying a life way past retirement. It is not so. In 1997 Thailand suffered a severe economic crunch and my business almost went down under. It took me many years to try to come back. Just as I thought I was climbing out of the black hole, another crisis hit two years ago. This time I am too old to fight, but I have no choice but to go on. I thought that God and I were very close. However, after the first crisis hit I sort of lost my faith along with my hope. After the second crisis hit, I thought that God had forsaken me. I all but lost my faith totally until one day a good friend gave me a book, *Never, Never Give Up*. At first I didn't want to read it. However, insisted by my friend, I did. I stayed up the whole night finishing the book. By morning I kneeled down and begged God to forgive me for my foolishness. I felt so ashamed for my behavior. I begged Him to accept me back. After I did that, I know that God has forgiven me. Now I am back to feeling close to Him again. I am so happy and grateful for this book. God is great!" (Thailand)

- "Thanks for being there when you are so much needed by all of us. After seven major operations I am beginning to walk again and help others which is the full purpose of my existence which Jesus Christ has set before me. Your book, *Never, Never Give Up*, stayed by my pillow along with my Bible while I was recuperating from these operations. When I re-read it, I was charged with peace and energy again. The pain diminishes and I can speak of God's infinite love and mercy to others who are facing similar trials. Thank you for writing this God-inspired book." (Florida)

- "Suicide has shown its face in my mind. I found myself falling deeper and deeper into the pit of hell. My life seemed so grim. I could not see where I could make a difference and was planning to believe that if I chose to leave this life it would not matter. When I received *Never, Never Give Up* I read the first three chapters that evening. When I arrived at page ninety, your verse changed my life. I want you to know that I have been delivered from this season of trial. I rededicated my life to the Lord and feel wonderful. Thank you so much for your work. Through our Lord you have saved my life. Thank you for my life back." (Texas)

Overcoming Fear

- "Thank you for sending your books to the Philippines. I was very blessed to read *Overcoming Fear.* This book explained the sources of fear and what I should do to overcome fear. It is really a blessing to know all of this information that helped me to overcome the fear I have felt all these years. I have cherished every chapter in the book. It has become food for my soul. Thank you so much for explaining all of this so well. I have learned that I should never be afraid of anyone because I can be absolutely certain that God lives in my heart. This is great assurance because I know that God is greater than anything I will ever face in this life. This book has been a great blessing in my life. God bless you both." (the Philippines)

- "I want to thank you immediately for your new book, *Overcoming Fear.* I have read every one of your books and given copies to many people, but I want to tell you that I believe this is your best book ever. I can hardly put it down. The day I received it I stayed up late, even though I was very tired, to read the first four chapters. The next morning I read two more chapters before going to work. This book is very inspiring. It gives me great peace. God's peace is so great that I cannot describe it. I have almost finished reading this book. When I am done, I will immediately read it again. Enclosed is a check for ten copies of this book plus a contribution to Lamplight Ministries. Thank you, Jack and Judy, for writing this wonderful book." (Massachusetts)

- "I want to thank you for publishing the book *Overcoming Fear.* I am reading mine for the second time. I cannot tell you how comforting it is. The way you have put information along with the right Bible verses is so truly helpful. As world conditions worsen, I can tell you that this book will be a constant companion alongside my Bible. I am so grateful for you both. Keep up the good work. You are making a big difference in peoples' lives. You have in mine." (Minnesota)

Victory Over Adversity

- "I am a pure and proud Dutchman married to a Tanzanian woman. I have had a lot of problems staying with an African wife in Europe. I love my wife so much, but the environment for my wife was not good enough in terms of getting a job. This affected us very much to the extent that I was even planning to relocate to Tanzania for the sake of my wife and children's future. Thank God that an angel was sent to me by the name of Jim who gave me a book, *Victory over Adversity*. This book is amazing and great. It contains the answers to my problems and is a great encouragement to me. As a Dutchman I find it very interesting to read a book with simple English. Putting the facts of this book into practice has changed my life greatly. I have found a new job. My wife has found a good job. The thoughts of relocating to Tanzania have faded. My faith has increased and my commitment to God has grown. I pray that God will bless the writers of this book and also the man who gave me this book. My wife and I are always reading this book. It is our source of strength." (Holland)

- "I praise God for His living Word. Thank you for the books that you have sent to China. You cannot imagine what *Victory over Adversity* did in my life as a young believer. Not only is the language clear and accessible, but the content is very rewarding. I learned a lot from this book. I now meditate day and night on the Word of God. I am in the presence of God often. I am confident that I can overcome any adversity in the precious name of Jesus Christ. May God bless you and fill you with His infinite grace, Mr. Jack and his wife." (China)

- "I am a 22-year-old college student in Thailand. My family is half Christian. My mother is a Christian whereas my father is a Buddhist. I am the eldest daughter of my parents with one younger brother and sister. All three of us have been baptized as Christians since birth. Frankly, I have never had much faith in God and always have had problems with both of my parents. I think that they don't understand me. They think I don't listen to them. Last month my mother was given a book, *Victory over Adversity,* by her friend. Out of curiosity I took the book and read it before she did. I could not put it down. For the first time I felt that God is real and is close to me. I cried and cried and felt sorry for my past behavior toward God and my parents. I went to my mother and apologized, to her great surprise. Now I go to church with her every Sunday. I am very thankful to my mother's friend who gave her this book and also to the writers of this book who have changed my life and brought me to God which my mother could not do. Thank you both!" (Thailand)

Exchange Your Worries for God's Perfect Peace

- "*Exchange Your Worries for God's Perfect Peace* is a masterpiece. I am reading this book to the people here in the Philippines. I saw tears flowing down their faces as I read them parts of this book. I must get this book translated into their language. I am reading this book for the second time. After 30 years in the ministry I have finally learned how to turn my worries over to God. I have learned more from this book in the last few months than I have ever learned in my life. I will not allow my copy of this book to leave my presence. I thank God for you." (the Philippines)

- "I just want to tell you how much I appreciate you and your excellent book, *Exchange Your Worries for God's Perfect Peace.* I have read all of your books several times each. I continually go back to refer to the notes I have made in your books. I have done this for close to 15 years and pages are falling out of your books. I read the Bible daily. Your books are a close second to the Bible. I have never found another Christian author who teaches me more about God's Word and speaks directly to my heart as your writings do. Thank you for helping me appreciate and respect the Word of God." (Wisconsin)

- "I was in despair struggling with my life and ministry. *Exchange Your Worries for God's Perfect Peace* has strengthened me and encouraged my heart. My country is often threatened by disasters. Your book and the Scripture in it has helped me to focus on God, no matter what circumstances I have experienced and will face in the future. The language in the book is very clear and easy to understand for someone like me who uses English as a second language. I have been blessed by reading this book. My faith in Jesus has increased. Thank you for sending this book to me. I thank God that I know you. You are a blessing." (Indonesia)

God's Joy Regardless of Circumstances

- "*God's Joy Regardless of Circumstances* came to me right on time. Being in prison for 20 years for a crime I didn't commit and then having to deal with severe family problems is not a morsel that is easy to swallow. My oldest daughter was pregnant and we were looking forward to having my first grandson born. We were very pained to learn that my daughter had to lose her baby. In the midst of dealing with this problem, you sent me a free copy of *God's Joy Regardless of Circumstances*. When I avidly started to read this book, my daughter underwent surgery, lost her baby and faced uncertainty and despair. *God's Joy Regardless of Circumstances* pulled us through. Thank you also for sending a free copy of this book to my daughter. May God continue blessing Lamplight Ministries." (Florida)

- "Many thanks for sending me *God's Joy Regardless of Circumstances*. This book has been a real stream in the desert that I have been able to drink from. I have been blessed tremendously by this book. My life has not been the same since I started reading it. I have used this book to help many people on my radio programme every

Sunday. Many people have given their lives to Christ because of these messages." (Zambia)

- "Only this year I faced a lot of challenges. As a result I became bitter at heart. The wonderful Scripture verses in *God's Joy Regardless of Circumstances* took away my bitterness. I am happy now. This book has instructed me how to handle any situation with God's joy. I now can see God's solution to my life challenges by the presence of God's joy inside me. Your God-given insight has given new meaning to my spiritual life. Thank you for the encouragement through your writings." (Lome-Togo West Africa)

God's Wisdom Is Available to You

- "I did not sleep last night after reading your book *God's Wisdom is Available to You.* Thank you for your wonderful work. Because of persecution against my ministry, I spent a considerable amount of time in the hospital because of depression. I am now well and healthy in Jesus' name. Thank you for your help. I will be teaching members of my church from key text in your book. Please be my mentor, teacher and counselor." (Ghana)

- "I thank God each and every day for Jack and Judy Hartman. When I started reading your book on wisdom, everything was going wrong in my life. This book revived my spirit and my faith in God. It has changed my life. The Bible used to be like Greek to me. Now I can read it and understand it. I can't put this book down because I know I need to absorb it. I'm going through it for a second time. This book is one of the best things that has ever happened to me. I thank you both and I thank God." (Florida)

- "You did a fantastic job on this book. It is an encyclopedia on God's wisdom. The writing style is just great. Many books don't bring the reader through the subject the way this book does. I'm very impressed with that. You have made it a real joy for me to study and re-digest Scripture. This book has been very good for me." (North Carolina)

A Close and Intimate Relationship with God

- "Your book, *A Close and Intimate Relationship with God,* is tremendous. I thought that I had a close relationship with God, but this book really opened my eyes. I now can see many things that I still need to do to be even closer to God. I couldn't put this book down. When I had to stop reading, I couldn't wait to get back to it the next day. Every chapter is filled with Scripture that is very helpful to me. I will be making many changes in my life as a result of reading this awesome book. Thank you and God bless you." (New Hampshire)

- "Thank you for giving me a copy of your book *A Close and Intimate Relationship with God.* This book is written so clearly that all instructions are to the point. My life has been greatly changed and refreshed. The presence of God has become very strong in my life. I am at peace trusting my God to meet every need. My mind is totally on God. I can clearly hear His voice. I am receiving guidance and direction from Him as a result of this book. I cannot afford to spend a day without reading this book. I carry it with me wherever I go." (Zambia)

- "Thank you for your book titled *A Close and Intimate Relationship with God.* This inspiring book helped me to draw closer to our heavenly Father. In Chapter 25 you said that Paul and Silas were praising God in prison. I was having a challenging day when I read this chapter. God spoke through your book to praise Him no matter what circumstances I faced. Thank you for that inspiration. The information on dying to self in the last chapter where Paul said that he dies daily really encouraged me. I am learning to do much better putting

God first, others second and myself last. Thank you at Lamplight Ministries for the thousands of people around the world that you are supporting. May the dear Lord bless you abundantly." (China)

Unshakable Faith in Almighty God

- "I thank God for the book *Unshakable Faith in Almighty God*. Because I am not indigenous Chinese, it is not easy to fellowship with the local Chinese. When I got this book I was able to see a way in the wilderness. It became my guide and light every day. When I was just about to give up Christianity, God at the right time provided this book to me. The truths and clear instruction in this book are direct from the throne of God. I am determined to move on with God come what may. I praise God that is He able to raise people we have never seen like Jack and Judy Hartman to speak into our lives through their publications. God bless the Hartman family. One day when Christ comes it will be exciting for them to see how they have influenced the world for God in Jesus' name. I am so grateful for these free books that cost a lot of money in publishing, printing and postage." (China)

- "I have been pastoring in Belgium for the past 15 years. In the past our church was flourishing and doing very well until late last year when my praise and worship leader decided to break away and form another church. This was a very big blow to us as a church. Most of our strong and committed members left the church with some of the church instruments. My wife almost gave up. She was discouraged. This also affected our finances. Pastor Jim gave me a book titled *Unshakable Faith in Almighty God*. Before I read this book my faith was shaken and I almost gave up. This book took me step by step to show me how to make my faith grow. You cannot read this book and remain the same. I have been using the book to preach to the few members that remain with us. In the past four months we have experienced revival. The anointing is so strong and the members have been strengthened so much through the preaching from this book. We are determined to not give up. God bless the Hartmans for being a blessing to us in Europe." (Belgium)

- "*Unshakable Faith in Almighty God* has amazed me. The language is so simple and very clear to understand. This book is powerful and life-changing. I will always hang on to this book. Brother Hartman, God's favour and wisdom are so great on your life. I believe this book is written on very heavy anointing from God. Your reward in heaven will be so great. All those who have sown seeds in your ministry should rejoice. When I wake up, I read this book. Before going to bed, I read it. I will continue to go through it again and again. Your ministry is a big blessing to me. You are always in our prayers." (Zambia)

How to Study the Bible
- "Your book, *How to Study the Bible*, is a gem. Since I became a Christian 41 years ago, I have studied the Bible using a variety of methods. Your method is simple and straightforward. It involves hard work, but the rewards are real. I have read several of your books and this book is the one I would highly recommend to any Christian because this book is the foundation. God bless you, brother." (England)
- "My wife and I are utilizing the Bible study method that you explained in *How to Study the Bible*. We are really growing spiritually as a result. Our old methods of study were not nearly as fruitful. Thank you for writing about your method." (Idaho)
- "I have read almost all of your books and they are outstanding. The one that blessed me the most was *How to Study the Bible*. The study part was excellent, but the

meditation chapters were very, very beneficial. I am indebted to you for sharing these. I purchased 30 copies to give to friends. Every earnest student of God's Word needs a copy." (Tennessee)

Increased Energy and Vitality

- "It is so great to meet Christians on the same wave length. In your book *Increased Energy and Vitality*, you are writing almost word for word in some cases what I have been saying to patients for almost 30 years." (Ohio)
- "Last year I obtained a copy of your book *Increased Energy and Vitality*. My wife and I have read and have in fact changed our ways of eating and drinking and exercising because of your influence. We thoroughly appreciate this God-centered message that is so well presented. I have enclosed an order for more of these books. We know many people we wish to help. This is the first step in spreading the news you have so generously put together. Thank you for your efforts. May God continue your leadership in writing, speaking and guidance." (Illinois)
- "I have benefited tremendously from reading and personally applying the principles learned from your book *Increased Energy and Vitality*. By applying your methods, I have gained additional energy especially during my low periods from 2:00 p.m. to 4:00 p.m. I highly recommend your book to others. Keep up the good work." (Florida)

100 Years from Today

- "*100 Years From Today* told me that going to church and doing good deeds won't get me to heaven. I believe in Jesus Christ. I believe He died for our sins and that He forgives us for what we did wrong. Heaven is where I belong. I am born again. I have a new life. This book has changed my life." (Florida)

- "I am writing to express my deep and profound appreciation for your book *100 Years from Today*. I recently began attending a Bible-based church where I found a copy of this book in their lending library. I read the book in one sitting, reading the words aloud to myself. Your book explained details from the Bible that I had not learned before. I thank you for taking the time and effort to write this book. My written words can never fully express how grateful I am to you. By my actions, a changed life and a deep sense of peace, I hope to bear fruit by helping others." (Massachusetts)
- "I find it hard to put *100 Years from Today* down. I read the whole book in a day and a half. I never knew how much pain and suffering Jesus went through to pay for my sins. I learned how much He loves us." (Florida)

Nuggets of Faith
- "Your books, tapes and meditation cards are really a blessing to me. They came at just the right time. I am preparing sermons on faith from *Nuggets of Faith*. I want the congregation to be constantly learning God's Word in order to have much more faith. I also have been encouraged personally through that book. It is awesome. Thank you for your powerful and inspiring publications." (Zambia)
- "We give *Nuggets of Faith* to people who are hospitalized, for birthdays, to saved and unsaved. Everyone who has received one tells us 'It's the best little book I've ever read. It's so clear and easy to understand.'" (Indiana)
- "I work as a store manager. Today I was told that I was no longer needed. Praise Jesus that only two months prior to this date I had accepted the Lord Jesus as my personal Lord and Savior. I have faith that the Lord was working to bring me to a new direction. I am writing to thank you for your excellent book *Nuggets of Faith*. The moment I

arrived home after having been dismissed, I received this book in the mail. I completed this short but awesome book in a little over two hours. It has helped my faith to grow stronger and I know that I will begin a great new journey tomorrow. God bless you." (New York)

Comments on our Scripture Meditation Cards

- "My back was hurting so badly that I couldn't get comfortable. I was miserable whether I sat or stood or laid down. I didn't know what to do. Suddenly I thought of the Scripture cards on healing that my husband had purchased. I decided to meditate on the Scripture in these cards. I was only on the second card when, all of a sudden, I felt heat go from my neck down through my body. The Lord had healed me. I never knew it could happen so fast. The pain has not come back." (Idaho)

- "My wife and I use your Scripture cards every day when we pray. I read the card for that day in English and then my wife repeats it in Norwegian. We then pray based upon the Scripture reference on that day's card. These cards have been very beneficial to us. We would like to see the Scripture cards published in the Norwegian language." (Norway)

- "Your Scripture cards have been very helpful to my wife and myself. We have taped them to the walls in our home and we meditate on them constantly. I also take four or five cards with me every day when I go to work. I meditate on them while I drive. The Scripture on these cards is a constant source of encouragement to us. We ask for permission to translate *Trust God for Your Finances*. This book is badly needed by the people in Turkey." (This permission was granted.) (Turkey)

- "My mom is 95 years old. She was in the Bergen-Belsen Concentration Camp in Germany from 1943 to 1945. She has always had a lot of worry and fear. My mother was helped greatly in overcoming this problem by your Scripture cards titled *Freedom from Worry and Fear*. She was helped so much that she asked me to order another set to give to a friend." (California)
- "I am overwhelmed about the revelations in your Scripture Meditation Cards. These Scripture cards have helped me so much that I cannot write enough on this sheet of paper. We have gone through a five-day programme in our church using the Scripture cards. My faith has increased tremendously. I no longer am submitting to my own will and desires, but I am now submitting to the will of God and it is so fantastic. God bless you, Jack and Judy Hartman." (Ghana)
- "I am very enthusiastic about your Scripture cards and your tape titled *Receive Healing from the Lord*. I love your tape. The clarity of your voice and your sincerity and compassion will encourage sick people. They can listen to this tape throughout the day, before they go to sleep at night, while they are driving to the doctor's office, in the hospital, etc. The tape is filled with Scripture and many good comments on Scripture. This cassette tape and your Scripture cards on healing are powerful tools that will help many sick people." (Tennessee) (NOTE: The ten cassette tapes for our Scripture Meditation Cards are available on 60 minute CDs as well.)
- "I meditate constantly on the healing cards and listen to your tape on healing over and over. Your voice is so soothing. You are a wonderful teacher. My faith is increasing constantly." (New Hampshire).

- "I thank God for you. I carry your Scripture Meditation Cards in my purse. The Scriptures you have chosen are all powerful. What a blessing to be able to meditate on the Word of God at any time, anywhere. Thank you for your hard work. The Scripture cards are a blessing to me." (Canada)

We offer you a substantial quantity discount

From the beginning of our ministry we have been led of the Lord to offer the same quantity discount to individuals that we offer to Christian bookstores. Each individual has a sphere of influence with a specific group of people. We believe that you know many people who need to learn the scriptural contents of our publications.

The Word of God encourages us to give freely to others. We encourage you to give selected copies of these publications to people you know who need help in the specific areas that are covered by our publications. See our order form for specific information on the quantity discounts that we make available to you so that you can share our books, Scripture Meditation Cards and CDs with others.

A request to our readers

If this book has helped you, we would like to receive your comments so that we can share them with others. Your comments can encourage other people to study our publications to learn from the scriptural contents of these publications.

When we receive a letter containing comments on any of our books, cassette tapes or Scripture Meditation Cards, we prayerfully take out excerpts from these letters. These selected excerpts are included in our newsletters and occasionally in our advertising and promotional materials.

If any of our publications have been a blessing to you, please share your comments with us so that we can share them with others. Tell us in your own words what a specific publication has meant to you and why you would recommend it to others. Please give as much specific information as possible. We prefer three or four paragraphs so that we can condense this into one paragraph.

Thank you for taking a few minutes of your time to encourage other people to learn from the scripture references in our publications.

Jack and Judy

ORDER FORM FOR BOOKS

Book Title	Quantity	Total
What Does God Say? ($18)	_____x $18 =	_____
Reverent Awe of God ($14)	_____x $14 =	_____
God's Plan for Your Life ($14)	_____x $14 =	_____
You Can Hear the Voice of God ($14)	_____x $14 =	_____
Effective Prayer ($14)	_____x $14 =	_____
God's Instructions for Growing Older ($14)	_____x $14 =	_____
A Close and Intimate Relationship with God ($14)	_____x $14 =	_____
God's Joy Regardless of Circumstances ($14)	_____x $14 =	_____
Victory Over Adversity ($14)	_____x $14 =	_____
Receive Healing from the Lord ($14)	_____x $14 =	_____
Unshakable Faith in Almighty God ($14)	_____x $14 =	_____
Exchange Your Worries for God's Perfect Peace ($14)	_____x $14 =	_____
God's Wisdom is Available to You ($14)	_____x $14 =	_____
Overcoming Fear ($14)	_____x $14 =	_____
Trust God For Your Finances ($14)	_____x $14 =	_____
What Will Heaven Be Like? ($14)	_____x $14 =	_____
Quiet Confidence in the Lord ($14)	_____x $14 =	_____
Never, Never Give Up ($14)	_____x $14 =	_____
Increased Energy and Vitality ($14)	_____x $14 =	_____
How to Study the Bible ($10)	_____x $10 =	_____
Nuggets of Faith ($10)	_____x $10 =	_____
100 Years From Today ($10)	_____x $10 =	_____

Price of books _____

Minus 40% discount for 5-9 books _____

Minus 50% discount for 10 or more books _____

Net price of order _____

Add 15% **before discount** for shipping and handling _____

Florida residents only, add 7% sales tax _____

Tax deductible contribution to Lamplight Ministries, Inc. _____

Enclosed check or money order (do not send cash) _____

(Foreign orders must be submitted in U.S. dollars.)

Please make check payable to **Lamplight Ministries, Inc.** and mail to:
PO Box 1307, Dunedin, FL 34697

MC____ Visa____ AmEx____ Disc.____ Card # _____

Exp Date _____ Signature _____

Name _____

Address _____

City _____

State or Province _____ Zip or Postal Code _____

Email _____ Website: _____

ORDER FORM FOR BOOKS

Book Title	Quantity	Total
What Does God Say? ($18)	_____ x $18 =	_____
Reverent Awe of God ($14)	_____ x $14 =	_____
God's Plan for Your Life ($14)	_____ x $14 =	_____
You Can Hear the Voice of God ($14)	_____ x $14 =	_____
Effective Prayer ($14)	_____ x $14 =	_____
God's Instructions for Growing Older ($14)	_____ x $14 =	_____
A Close and Intimate Relationship with God ($14)	_____ x $14 =	_____
God's Joy Regardless of Circumstances ($14)	_____ x $14 =	_____
Victory Over Adversity ($14)	_____ x $14 =	_____
Receive Healing from the Lord ($14)	_____ x $14 =	_____
Unshakable Faith in Almighty God ($14)	_____ x $14 =	_____
Exchange Your Worries for God's Perfect Peace ($14)	_____ x $14 =	_____
God's Wisdom is Available to You ($14)	_____ x $14 =	_____
Overcoming Fear ($14)	_____ x $14 =	_____
Trust God For Your Finances ($14)	_____ x $14 =	_____
What Will Heaven Be Like? ($14)	_____ x $14 =	_____
Quiet Confidence in the Lord ($14)	_____ x $14 =	_____
Never, Never Give Up ($14)	_____ x $14 =	_____
Increased Energy and Vitality ($14)	_____ x $14 =	_____
How to Study the Bible ($10)	_____ x $10 =	_____
Nuggets of Faith ($10)	_____ x $10 =	_____
100 Years From Today ($10)	_____ x $10 =	_____

Price of books _____

Minus 40% discount for 5-9 books _____

Minus 50% discount for 10 or more books _____

Net price of order _____

Add 15% **before discount** for shipping and handling _____

Florida residents only, add 7% sales tax _____

Tax deductible contribution to Lamplight Ministries, Inc. _____

Enclosed check or money order (do not send cash) _____

(Foreign orders must be submitted in U.S. dollars.)

Please make check payable to **Lamplight Ministries, Inc**. and mail to:
PO Box 1307, Dunedin, FL 34697

MC____ Visa____ AmEx____ Disc.____ Card # _____

Exp Date _____ Signature _____

Name _____

Address _____

City _____

State or Province _____ Zip or Postal Code _____

Email _____ Website: _____

ORDER FORM FOR SCRIPTURE MEDITATION CARDS AND CDs

SCRIPTURE MEDITATION CARDS	QUANTITY	PRICE
Find God's Will for Your Life ($5)	_____	_____
Financial Instructions from God ($5)	_____	_____
Freedom from Worry and Fear ($5)	_____	_____
A Closer Relationship with the Lord ($5)	_____	_____
Our Father's Wonderful Love ($5)	_____	_____
Receive Healing from the Lord ($5)	_____	_____
Receive God's Blessing in Adversity ($5)	_____	_____
Enjoy God's Wonderful Peace ($5)	_____	_____
God is Always with You ($5)	_____	_____
Continually Increasing Faith in God ($5)	_____	_____

CDs	QUANTITY	PRICE
Find God's Will for Your Life ($10)	_____	_____
Financial Instructions from God ($10)	_____	_____
Freedom from Worry and Fear ($10)	_____	_____
A Closer Relationship with the Lord ($10)	_____	_____
Our Father's Wonderful Love ($10)	_____	_____
Receive Healing from the Lord ($10)	_____	_____
Receive God's Blessing in Adversity ($10)	_____	_____
Enjoy God's Wonderful Peace ($10)	_____	_____
God is Always with You ($10)	_____	_____
Continually Increasing Faith in God ($10)	_____	_____

TOTAL PRICE _____

Minus 40% discount for 5-9 Scripture Cards and CDs _____

Minus 50% discount for 10 or more Scripture Cards and CDs _____

Net price of order _____

Add 15% **before discount** for shipping and handling _____

Florida residents only, add 7% sales tax _____

Tax deductible contribution to Lamplight Ministries, Inc. _____

Enclosed check or money order (do not send cash) _____

(Foreign orders must be submitted in U.S. dollars.)

Please make check payable to **Lamplight Ministries, Inc**. and mail to:
PO Box 1307, Dunedin, FL 34697

MC____ Visa____ AmEx____ Disc.____ Card # _____

Exp Date _____ Signature _____

Name _____

Address _____

City _____

State or Province _____ Zip or Postal Code _____

Email _____ Website: _____

ORDER FORM FOR SCRIPTURE MEDITATION CARDS AND CDs

SCRIPTURE MEDITATION CARDS	QUANTITY	PRICE
Find God's Will for Your Life ($5)		
Financial Instructions from God ($5)		
Freedom from Worry and Fear ($5)		
A Closer Relationship with the Lord ($5)		
Our Father's Wonderful Love ($5)		
Receive Healing from the Lord ($5)		
Receive God's Blessing in Adversity ($5)		
Enjoy God's Wonderful Peace ($5)		
God is Always with You ($5)		
Continually Increasing Faith in God ($5)		

CDs	QUANTITY	PRICE
Find God's Will for Your Life ($10)		
Financial Instructions from God ($10)		
Freedom from Worry and Fear ($10)		
A Closer Relationship with the Lord ($10)		
Our Father's Wonderful Love ($10)		
Receive Healing from the Lord ($10)		
Receive God's Blessing in Adversity ($10)		
Enjoy God's Wonderful Peace ($10)		
God is Always with You ($10)		
Continually Increasing Faith in God ($10)		

TOTAL PRICE

Minus 40% discount for 5-9 Scripture Cards and CDs _____

Minus 50% discount for 10 or more Scripture Cards and CDs _____

Net price of order _____

Add 15% **before discount** for shipping and handling _____

Florida residents only, add 7% sales tax _____

Tax deductible contribution to Lamplight Ministries, Inc. _____

Enclosed check or money order (do not send cash) _____

(Foreign orders must be submitted in U.S. dollars.)

Please make check payable to **Lamplight Ministries, Inc**. and mail to:
PO Box 1307, Dunedin, FL 34697

MC____ Visa____ AmEx____ Disc.____ Card # _____

Exp Date _____ Signature _____

Name _____

Address _____

City _____

State or Province _____ Zip or Postal Code _____

Email _____ Website: _____

Made in the USA
San Bernardino, CA
07 December 2017